A nightingale falls in love
with the Rose.
The whole love affair begins
with just one look from God.

Yunus Emre

Love is a Fire

Love is a Fire

The Sufi's Mystical Journey Home

LLEWELLYN VAUGHAN-LEE

THE GOLDEN SUFI CENTER

First published in the United States in 2000 by
The Golden Sufi Center
P.O. Box 456
Point Reyes Station, California 94956
www.goldensufi.org

©2000, 2020 by The Golden Sufi Center.

Fifth printing 2020.

Printed in the USA.

Library of Congress Cataloging in Publication Data

Vaughan-Lee, Llewellyn.
    Love is a fire/Llewellyn Vaughan-Lee.
        p. cm.
    Includes bibliographical references and index.
    ISBN 1-890350-03-6 (pbk. : alk. paper)
    1. Sufism. 2. Spiritual life. I. Title.

    BP189 .V39 2000
    297.4--dc21

ISBN 10: 1-890350-03-6
ISBN 13: 978-1-890350-03-1

CONTENTS

PREFACE

Throughout this book, in an effort to maintain continuity and simplicity of text, God, the Great Beloved, is referred to as He. Of course, the Absolute Truth is neither masculine nor feminine. As much as It has a divine masculine side, so It has an awe-inspiring feminine aspect.

The use of the pronoun also evokes the primacy of the love affair with the Beloved on the Sufi path. Central to Sufism is this greatest mystery of the heart's love affair with God, that leads the lover from the illusion of separation from God to the mystery of divine union, oneness with God. The Beloved is both beyond masculine and feminine, but also comes to be experienced as the divine lover within our heart and soul, within every breath of our being.

INTRODUCTION

In the whole of the universe there are only two, the lover and the Beloved.

Bhai Sahib

The song of love is in every heart. Each of us longs to be loved, loved by a mother, a lover, a friend, a husband or wife. We long to be touched, to be held, to be embraced, to be understood, to be needed. We need to know that we are loved and we need to love in return. Love is the primal music of life, the song of creation, the fabric of being human.

For some the need for love is buried beneath other needs, beneath psychological problems or other patterns. Their feelings may be caught in a tangle of fears or insecurities, hidden or inaccessible. Some people are frightened by their need for love, or by its intangible nature, and seek instead material security; they cover a deeper hunger with a greed for money or possessions. Some people seem to run from love, seeking pain or rejection as a way to avoid love's vulnerability. And some people are drawn by love, drawn deeper and deeper within themselves to the core of their being. They are drawn to the essence of love, to the root of the root of loving which is the soul's love for God and God's love for the creation.

Those who are drawn to the root of love are mystics. Mystics are not satisfied with the surface patterns of love, with the emotional tangles and insecurities of human loving. They seek a purer wine, a more potent passion. They need the essence of love, its divine substance. For centuries mystics have been walking secret paths to love, paths that lead to the shores of love's infinite ocean. Some of these travelers became known as Sufis, wayfarers on the path of love. Sufis are lovers of God, going Home to their heart's Beloved. Because Sufis are lovers of God, their relationship with God is that of lover and Beloved.

Some souls need to know that they love God. They are drawn into this love as a moth is drawn to the flame. There is a spark within the heart of the lover that is ignited by love and can only be satisfied by union with God. But how does one live this love affair of the heart of hearts, how does one make this journey Home? For centuries Sufis have tried to describe the way love draws us back to God. They have made maps of the path across the desert of separation and described the provisions we need for this journey: the practices and qualities that will enable the lover to go Home to the Beloved.

Each in our own way we are drawn to God. Each in our own way we make the journey from duality back to oneness. There are many different Sufi paths, reflecting the different needs of wayfarers. Some are taken into the arena of their heart through music and dance, while for others silence is the only way. But underneath there is the one note of the soul's longing for God, the cry that comes from the depths of the heart and reminds us of our real Home, of where we truly belong. Every Sufi path awakens this cry and helps us to follow it. The heart's cry is a golden thread that leads us through the maze of our own psyche as well as through the distractions of the world.

Longing takes us back to God, takes the lover back into the arms of the Beloved. This is the ancient path of the mystic, of those who are destined to make the journey to the further shores of love. Why we are called to this quest is always a mystery, for the ways of the heart cannot be understood by the mind. Love draws us back to love, and longing is the fire that purifies us. Sufis know the secrets of love, of the way love takes and transforms us. They are the people of love who have kept alive the mysteries of divine loving, of what is hidden within the depths of the human being.

Since the beginning of time, long, long before they were called Sufis, the people of love have carried this wisdom for humanity. Sufism is the ancient wisdom of love, a wisdom that is as free as the sunshine. Sufis belong only to love, and in their essence are free of the constrictions of outer form. Just as love has no form, so Sufism is "Truth without form." At different times Sufism appears in different outer forms, according to the need of the time and the place and the people. But under the clothing of the mystic there is only the oneness of love, a oneness that cannot be limited or constricted.

The heart has many secrets, and its greatest mystery is how it can contain the wonders of God. The heart is the meeting place of lover and Beloved, the place where the lover dissolves into love. Those who are drawn into the arena of love, of a love that carries the fragrance of what is Real, can learn from the Sufis. They can follow the footsteps of these pilgrims of the heart, this band of lovers who have tasted the sweetness that was before honey or bee. Sufis tell us of this journey, and their maps outline the stages along the way. Their wisdom of love is alive and belongs to those who have been awakened by love and need to find their way back to their Beloved.

Sufis all sing the one song, that of lover and Beloved. The Beloved looks into the heart of the lover and ignites it with the spark of remembrance, with the call for the journey. This spark becomes a fire that burns us, that empties us of everything except love. Through the fire of love we come to know the essence of love, the greatest secret hidden within every cell of creation. Finding what we really are, we become lost in the mystical truth of humanity, that there is nothing other than God.

1. THE PATH OF LOVE

You are a Sufi when your heart is as soft and as warm as wool.

traditional

LOVERS OF GOD

Sufism is a path of love. The Sufi is a traveler on the path of love, a wayfarer journeying back to God through the mysteries of the heart. For the Sufi the relationship to God is that of lover and Beloved, and Sufis are also known as lovers of God. The journey to God takes place within the heart, and for centuries Sufis have been traveling deep within themselves, into the secret chamber of the heart where lover and Beloved share the ecstasy of union.

There are some people for whom spiritual life has to be a love affair, a passionate affair of the soul. This tremendous love affair takes place within the heart, and is one of the greatest mysteries of being human. To love God and to be loved by God, to experience the depth and intimacy of this relationship, is a secret long known to the Sufis. Within the heart we come closer and closer to our Beloved, so close that finally there is no separation as the lover merges into the Beloved, the lover becomes lost in love. Step by step we walk along the path of love until finally we are taken by love into love; we are taken by God to God, and then there is no going back, only a deepening and deepening of this love affair of the soul. This is the ancient journey from separation to union, the journey from our own self back to a state of oneness with God.

On this journey love is the power that will take us Home. Love is the most powerful force in the universe and it resides within the heart of each of us. But this love needs to be awakened. The heart needs to be activated so that it can come to know its primordial passion, this link of love that runs through the world and is our own essence.

Since the beginning of time there have been masters of love, spiritual teachers who understood the ways of love, how to activate and channel this latent power within the human being. They carry the knowledge of how to awaken the longing that the soul has for God and help the lover live this longing, of how to allow this longing to fulfill itself so that the lover comes to experience nearness, intimacy, and finally union with God. This is the ancient wisdom of love, how to activate the heart, how to work with the currents of love so that the human being is taken back to God. And this is the wisdom of the Sufis, the ancient path of love that has always been here, long, long before they were called Sufis.

There is a story about a group of mystics, a band of lovers of God, who were called the Kamal Posh. Kamal Posh means blanket wearers, for their only possession was one blanket which they wore as a covering during the day and used as a blanket at night. As the story goes they traveled throughout the ancient world from prophet to prophet but no one could satisfy them. Every prophet told them to do this or to do that, and this did not satisfy them. Then one day, at the time of Muhammad, the Prophet was seated together with his companions when he said that in a certain number of days the men of the Kamal Posh would be coming. So it happened that in that number of days this group of Kamal Posh came to the Prophet Muhammad. And when they were with him, he said nothing, but the Kamal Posh were completely satisfied. Why were they satisfied? Because he created love in their hearts, and when love is created, what dissatisfaction can there be?

Sufism is the ancient wisdom of the heart. It is not limited by time or place or form. It always was and it always will be. There will always be lovers of God. And the Kamal Posh recognized that Muhammad knew the mysteries of the heart. They stayed with the Prophet and were assimilated into Islam. According to this story the Kamal Posh became the mystical element of Islam. And later these wayfarers became known as Sufis, perhaps in reference to the white woolen blanket, *sûf*, which they wore, or as an indication of their purity of heart, *safâ*, for they were also known as the pure of heart.

These lovers of God followed Islam, and observed the teachings of the Qur'an, but from a mystical point of view. For example, in the Qur'an there is a saying that God, Allâh, is nearer to us than our jugular vein (Sûra 50:16). For the Sufis this saying speaks about the mystical experience of nearness with God. The Sufi relates to God not as a judge, nor as a father figure, nor as the creator, but as our own Beloved, who is so close, so near, so tender. In the states of nearness the lover experiences an intimacy with the Beloved which carries the softness and ecstasy of love.

We all long to be loved, we all long to be nurtured, to be held, and we look for it in another; we seek a man or woman who can fulfill us. But the mystic knows the deeper truth, that no other person can ever answer our real needs. Maybe for a while an outer lover can appear to give us the love and support we crave, but an external lover will always be limited. Only within the heart can our deepest desires, our most passionate needs, be met, totally and completely. In moments of mystical intimacy with God we are given everything we could want, and more than we believe possible. He is closer to us than ourself to ourself, and He loves us with the completeness that belongs only to God.

Another passage from the Qur'an that carries a mystical meaning is the "verse of light" from Sûra 24, which contains the phrase, "light upon light, Allâh guides to His light whom He will." The Sufis have interpreted the words "light upon light" as describing the mystery of how His light hidden within our own heart rises up to God, giving us the longing and light we need for the journey. He awakens the lamp of divine light within the hearts of those who believe in the oneness of God. For the Sufi this light is a living reality that is felt as love, tenderness, and also the guidance that is necessary to help us on the way. His light takes us back to Him, from the pain of separation to the embrace of union.

Not only the Qur'an, but also the *hadîth*, the sayings attributed to the Prophet, often carry an inner meaning for the Sufi. One of the best known is "He who knows himself knows his Lord." This *hadîth* refers to the whole mystery of self-knowledge, of going within yourself, discovering your real nature, not what you think you are but what you really are. Sufism is a path of love and also a journey to self-knowledge, of carrying the light of consciousness into the core of our being. The spiritual journey is always inward, a gradual process of self-discovery as you realize the real wonder of being human. The wayfarer makes the most difficult and courageous of journeys, turning away from the outer world of illusion, and turning back to God, not as an idea but as a living reality that exists within the heart. This is a journey of self-revelation, a painful process of leaving behind our illusory nature, the ego, and entering into the arena of our true Self. And as another *hadîth* explicitly states, on this journey you have to "die before you die": before you can experience the innermost state of union with God, the ego has to be sacrificed; you have to be burnt, consumed by the fire of divine love.

FRIENDS OF GOD

In the early days of Sufism very little was written down; there were just luminaries, saints, friends of God, *walî*, who lived their own spiritual passion, their deepest devotion. One such saint was Râbi'a, a woman who was born into slavery, but whose owner was so impressed by the intensity of her devotion that he gave her her freedom. She became known for stressing the love that exists between the mystic and God. Always looking towards God, she cared for nothing that might distract from or interfere with this relationship. She was once asked, "Do you love God?" "Yes," she replied. "Do you hate the devil?" "No, my love of God gives me no time to hate the devil."

Râbi'a's prayer emphasizes the mystical rejection of everything but God: "Oh Lord, whatever share of this world thou dost bestow, bestow it on thine enemies. And whatever share of the next world doth thou giveth me, give it to thy friends. Thou art enough for me." An outer love affair may give us a semblance of fulfillment, but the intense inner love that belongs to the mystical relationship with God gives us a fulfillment that is total and absolute. Until you have tasted the degree of this inner fulfillment, you hardly dare dream that it is possible. But as the wayfarer walks along the path, as the lover comes closer to her Beloved, this fulfillment gets deeper and deeper, more and more complete; and you know, with a certainty that is born of experience, that only the Beloved can give you what you need. In the words of Râbi'a, "Thou art enough for me."

For the Sufi everything is given through love, within the heart. And it is given because our Beloved wills: "Allâh guides to Allâh whom He wills." The work of the wayfarer is really a work of preparation, to empty the cup of oneself so that He can fill it with the wine of love, the intoxicating substance of His love for us. The mystic knows that the only obstacle between us and our Beloved is our own self, as the tenth-century Sufi al-Hallâj passionately expressed:

> Between You and me there lingers an "it is I"
> which torments me.
> Ah! lift through mercy this "it is I"
> from between us both.

The lover longs to burn in the fire of love until he is empty, so that his Beloved can fill his heart with the wine of divine remembrance, with the taste of nearness, with the intimacies of love. He calls us to Him and we turn away from the world back to our Beloved, so that He can reveal the secret He has placed within our hearts, the wonder of oneness, the innermost union of lover and Beloved. Again to quote al-Hallâj, "I am He whom I love, He whom I love is me."

As mystics we burn with the fire of divine love that He has ignited within our heart. He calls us to Him and we respond, turning away from the world, turning away from our ego, to the deeper mystery hidden within the heart. And we make this journey, this sacrifice, because it is His will, because He has looked within our heart.

Someone came to Râbi'a and asked, "I have committed many sins; if I turn in penitence towards God, will He turn in mercy towards me?" "No," she replied, "first He must look upon you, then you can turn towards Him."

We are so easily identified only with our own effort and our own will that we have forgotten the primal truth of His need for us, His love for us: that He guides us back to Him because He wills. This is why the Sufi attaches such importance to surrender, and Islam means "surrender." The mystic walks a path of surrender, giving up his will, his own self, to the mysteries of love, drawn on this journey by the power of His love for us that He has awakened within our heart. The great ninth-century Sufi, Bâyezîd Bistâmî, came to realize this truth:

> At the beginning I was mistaken in four respects. I concerned myself to remember God, to know Him, to love Him and to seek Him. When I had come to the end I saw that He had remembered me before I remembered Him, that His knowledge of me had preceded my knowledge of Him, that His love towards me had existed before my love to Him and He had sought me before I sought Him.

His love towards us is the fundamental core of our existence, and of our spiritual quest. The whole of Sufism can be summed up in the saying in the Qur'an, "He loves them and they love Him" (Sûra 5:54). Within the heart the lover knows that this is the essence of her relationship with God: His love for us awakens our love for Him, His love draws us back to Him. The whole path is this drama of love being enacted within our heart and within our whole life.

ONENESS AND ANNIHILATION

Central to love is the quality of oneness. Love belongs to oneness and draws us towards oneness. We experience this in a human love affair. When our love for another draws us closer to that person, we want to get nearer and nearer, until in the moment of sexual union we are taken out of ourself into the bliss of ecstasy. Love for God awakens the memory of oneness that is stamped into the heart, and the path takes us into this arena. Bâyezîd Bistâmî was one of those God-intoxicated mystics who realized this essential oneness, the unity of God and man. Drunk with the wine of love, he exclaimed, "Under my garments there is nothing but God."

In the outer world we are so caught in duality, in separation from God, that we don't even know how we hunger for oneness. We have forgotten that we belong to God and that He is our own essential nature, the core of our being. But there are those in whom this memory is awakened, and, like the moth attracted by the candle, they are drawn into the fire of love, the fire that will burn away their own separate self, until all that remains is love.

The Sufis have been known as the people of the secret because they carry this secret of love, the oneness of lover and Beloved. Inwardly the cost of realizing oneness is always oneself, though some Sufis have had to pay a more physical price. Al-Hallâj was martyred for proclaiming *anâ'l-haqq* ("I am the Absolute Truth"). When he was executed, one of his fellow Sufis, Shiblî, said, "God gave you access to one of His secrets, but because you made it public He made you taste the blade." Through al-Hallâj the mysteries of love became known in the marketplace and the mosque. Love's martyr, he was prepared to pay the ultimate price, but he also knew that the physical world is only a veil of separation. Just before his death he exclaimed, "My God, here am I now in the dwelling place of my desires."

There is a Sufi saying that nothing is possible in love without death, and al-Hallâj knew and lived this. He said, "When Truth has taken hold of a heart, She empties it of all but Herself! When God attaches Himself to a man, He kills in him all else but Himself." The Sufis call this process of dying to oneself *fanâ*, annihilation. In the fire of love we are burnt, and through this burning the ego learns to surrender, to die to its own notion of supremacy. The lover learns to give herself totally to her Beloved, without thought or care for herself, until she can say, "The Beloved is living, the lover is dead." In this ultimate love affair we die to ourself, and this death is a painful process, because the ego, the "I," does not easily give up its notion of supremacy.

When I first came to the path I was given a taste of *fanâ*, of this annihilation of myself, although at the time I did not understand the experience. One evening I was invited to a talk on the spiritual dimension of mathematics. Sitting in front of me was a white-haired old lady, and after the talk I was introduced to her by a friend. This old lady, who was to be my teacher, gave me one look from her piercing blue eyes and I had the physical experience of becoming just a speck of dust on the floor. At the time I was an arrogant nineteen-year old and I thought I knew a lot about spirituality. I had read many books and had been practicing meditation and *hatha yoga*. But at that instant it all fell away and I became nothing. Years later I understood that it was a foretaste of the path, that the disciple has to become "less than a speck of dust at the feet of the teacher." But at the time I was just left in a state of bewilderment so profound I did not even think about it.

Sufism is a living mystical system. The great Sufis from the past have left us glimpses, the footprints of their journey. But over the centuries this wisdom of love has been passed from heart to heart, from culture to culture. After meeting this white-haired Russian lady I went to the small, North-London studio apartment where she lived and held meditation meetings. I experienced the love that comes from those who have given themselves totally to love, who are immersed in the soul's love affair with God. The path took me and transformed me, softened and emptied me. And always there was the sense of this ancient tradition of the lovers of God, stretching back to the beginning of time, and yet eternally present.

Sufism is for those who need a path that lives the primacy of love, who need to make the journey from separation to union, from the isolation of their own self to the intoxicating intimacy of their heart's Beloved. The path of love is a fire within the heart that burns away the veils of separation, emptying us of ourself so that we can come to experience our innermost state of union. The Beloved ignites the spark that becomes this fire because He wants us to come Home, to make the greatest journey, the soul's journey back to God. He wants us to know our true nature and to share with us the secret of His love, His hidden face. The mystery of "He loves them and they love Him" is so simple, so pure, so much a part of us and yet so easily forgotten. Sadly, in our culture we look for complexity and forget this primal mystery hidden within our own heart. Yet this is the mystery that the Sufis have long understood, the secret they hold in trust for mankind.

IBN 'ARABÎ AND JALALUDDIN RÛMÎ

Another great Sufi was Ibn 'Arabî, who was born in the twelfth century in Spain. Ibn 'Arabî was one of the few Sufis who didn't have a spiritual teacher. Instead, he said, he was initiated by Khidr. Khidr is a very important Sufi figure, who represents direct revelation. Mystics are not satisfied with hearing about God, with listening to other people's experiences; they are driven to realize God as a living reality within their own heart. And Khidr is the archetypal figure who gives the Sufi access to this direct revelation. Khidr is also known as the Green Man, and he usually appears in dreams as someone quite ordinary; you don't know that it is Khidr until he has gone.

Ibn 'Arabî had his first mystical experiences, his first immersion in the oneness of God, when he was quite young. He wrote over four hundred books, but at the core of his mystical teaching is the idea of the unity of being, that everything is one and everything is a part of God. Everything is God; He is the cause of every-thing, the essence of everything, and the substance of everything. There is no other existence than He. Ibn 'Arabî writes:

> When the mystery—of realizing that the mystic is one with the Divine—is revealed to you, you will understand that you are no other than God and that you have continued and will continue.... Then you will see all your actions to be His actions and your essence to be His essence.... There is nothing except His Face "whithersoever you turn, there is the Face of God."

Ibn 'Arabî became known as the greatest sheikh (sheikh is the term for a Sufi teacher). And he also became known as the "pole of knowledge" for the tremendous mystical understanding and insights he left behind. For example, he wrote about the importance of the imagination as a way of transcending the physical world and gaining access to the inner world of archetypal images. In recent years this knowledge of his has been rediscovered and forms the basis of revaluing this faculty of the imagination, a faculty which has been sadly rejected by our belief in rationalism.

Four years after Ibn 'Arabî's death in 1240, a meeting took place that was to inspire some of the world's greatest writings on mystical love. A theology professor was walking home from school when he met a ragged dervish. The professor was Jalaluddin Rûmî and the dervish, Shams-i Tabrîz. According to one story Rûmî fell at Shams' feet and renounced his religious teaching when the dervish recited these verses:

> If knowledge does not liberate the self from the self
> then ignorance is better than such knowledge.

Shams-i Tabrîz was the spark that ignited the fire of divine love within Rûmî, who summed up his life in the two lines:

> And the result is not more than these three words:
> I burnt, and burnt, and burnt.

Shams had awakened in him a fire that could only be satisfied with union, with the ecstatic loss of the self in the presence of the Beloved. And Rûmî knew how precious is this fire, this burning within the heart:

It is burning of the heart I want; this burning
   which is everything,
More precious than a worldly empire, because
   it calls God secretly, in the night.

Shams was the divine sun that had lighted Rûmî's
life. But one day Shams disappeared, possibly sensing
the jealousy of Rûmî's students and family. Rûmî was
distraught, but then he heard news that Shams was in
Damascus, and he sent his son, Sultân Walad, to bring
him back. When Shams returned Rûmî fell at his feet,
and once more they became inseparable, such that "no
one knew who was the lover and who was the beloved."
But again the jealousy of Rûmî's students and his younger
son destroyed their physical closeness. Again Shams
disappeared, possibly murdered. Rûmî was consumed
with grief, lost alone in the ocean of love.

But from the terrible pain of outer separation and
loss was born an inner union as he found his beloved
within his own heart. Inwardly united with Shams, the
theology professor was transformed into love's poet.
Rûmî knew the pain of love and the deepest purpose
of this fire within the heart, how it empties the human
being and fills him with the wine of love:

Love is here like the blood in my veins and skin
He has annihilated me and filled me only with Him
His fire has penetrated all the atoms of my body
Of "me" only my name remains; the rest is Him.

Rûmî became the poet of lovers, expressing the
crazy passion of the soul's desire for God. He knew that
lovers are madmen, gamblers, fools prepared to suffer
the deepest devastation for their invisible Beloved. He

spoke of the mystery that draws us into this burning, blissful obliteration:

> Love is a madman,
> working his wild schemes,
> tearing off his clothes, running
> through the mountains, drinking poison
> and now quietly choosing annihilation.

Rûmî's words, spoken centuries ago, ring in the soul of every lover, every wayfarer who seeks to follow this passion that is in the innermost of our being, the pathway in the soul that leads back to the Beloved. That Rûmî is the world's most popular poet today speaks of the need we have to hear these stories of divine love, to hear from a master of love how the heart can sing, cry, and burn with passion for God. Our culture may bombard us with material values but there is an inward hunger for what is real, for a love affair that belongs to the soul and not to the personality. Rûmî covers the spectrum of divine love: the haunting cry of the reed flute suffering separation from the reed bed, the laughter of lovers, the need to be naked, how "the mystic dances in the sun, hearing music others don't." With the language of love he tells us of the mystery of things, a mystery so lacking in our contemporary world. He reminds us of an unlived sorrow and an uncontainable joy, of the limitless horizon of the heart and the need for our heart's true Friend.

SUFI ORDERS

Rûmî was not only the greatest Sufi poet, but he also founded the Mevlevî order, often known as the

Whirling Dervishes due to their beautiful whirling dance, in which the dancers rotate like the planets turning around the sun. The founding of the different Sufi orders was an important part in the development of Sufism. In the early days of Sufism, small groups would gather around particular teachers, and by the eleventh century these groups had formed into spiritual orders, *tarîqas*, each order bearing the name of its founder.

The first order to emerge was the Qâdiryyah, founded by al-Jîlânî in the twelfth century in Baghdad. Jîlânî was an ascetic, a missionary, and a teacher, and became one of the most popular saints in the Islamic world. Other orders followed: the Suhrawardiyya, named after Suhrawardî, which spread into India and Afghanistan; the Rifâ'iyya order founded by Ahmad ar-Rifâ'î, which spread through Egypt and Syria and until the fifteenth century was one of the most popular orders. They were also known as the Howling Dervishes because they practiced a loud *dhikr* (*dhikr*, like *mantra*, is the repetition of a sacred phrase or name of God). They also became notorious for strange practices like eating snakes, cutting themselves with swords, and dancing in fire without being hurt.

In total contrast is the sobriety associated with the Naqshbandiyya, named after Bahâ ad-dîn Naqshband (d. 1390), but started by 'Abd'l-Khâliq al-Ghujduwânî (d. 1220). The Naqshbandis are also known as the Silent Sufis because they practice a silent rather than vocal *dhikr*. Bahâ ad-dîn said "God is silent and is most easily reached in silence." The Naqshbandiyya do not engage in *samâ*, sacred music or dance, and do not dress differently from ordinary people. Another aspect of the Naqshbandi path is the *suhbat*, the close relationship of master and disciple. The order was very powerful in

Central Asia from the thirteenth to the fifteenth century, and also spread throughout India.

Each order has its particular practices; some use music and dance, while others stress silence. But central to each *tarîqa* is the spiritual chain of succession stretching from sheikh to sheikh back to the founder of the order. Through this spiritual chain is transmitted the energy of the path, the power that is needed to take the wayfarer Home. The white-haired old lady whom I met when I was nineteen, and who gave me that look with her piercing blue eyes, was a representative of the Naqshbandi order. After the death of her husband, when she was in her fifties, she had gone to India where she met a Sufi master, who liked to be called Bhai Sahib. Bhai Sahib means elder brother, because traditionally the Sufi sheikh is "without a face, without a name." Sufis do not believe in personality worship, or in idealizing the teacher. The teacher is just a guide, a stepping stone from the world of illusion to the world of reality. Bhai Sahib trained her according to his system, and she was the first Western woman to be given this ancient spiritual training of the Naqshbandis.

She stayed with him for a number of years, undergoing an intense spiritual training, which she recorded as a diary. When she met him he told her to keep a diary of her experiences, and to keep a record of her dreams. Later he said, "I am not going to teach you anything. If I teach you things you will forget them. Instead I will give you experiences." Sufism is a path of experiences, in which the very inner substance of the individual is totally changed. Later, her diaries became a book, *Daughter of Fire* (*Chasm of Fire* in its abridged version), the first written record of this spiritual training. It tells of how love is created within the heart, how this divine love is experienced as burning longing, and the slow and painful process of purification that grinds down the ego until the disciple surrenders totally to the Beloved, to the currents of love that take her Home.

After Bhai Sahib's death in 1966 she returned to England, and brought this spiritual system to the West. When I met Irina Tweedie, or Mrs. Tweedie as she liked to be known, she had a small meditation group, just a few friends meeting twice a week. Meeting her, being in her presence, I knew that *she knew*, that she lived the secret for which I longed. This knowledge had nothing to do with words, but was stamped into the very core of her being and radiated from every cell. In her presence this mysterious path was alive, an ancient transmission of love that is from *soul to soul*, from *essence to essence*. Sufism is this transmission of love, a process of awakening the heart as an organ of direct perception: "*light upon light*, in Thy light shall we see light."

Mrs. Tweedie's small North-London room became my home from home, a space of reality in a world of illusion, a place where the heart was given precedence. We meditated and drank tea, she spoke of her teacher, and we shared dreams. Sufis believe in dreams, in the wisdom and guidance that they hold. And always beneath the surface of this company of friends, the primal mystery of being human was present, the secret of secrets, the heart's knowledge of its Beloved. Sufis are lovers of God; they live the truth that in the whole of the universe there are only two, the lover and the Beloved: "He loves them and they love Him."

I grew up in this atmosphere of love and the invisible presence of the path. Years later I had a dream in which I was told that I had been "made soft by a very hard system"; something within me had been softened by the love that was given, and yet the hardness of the system was always there, a path that pushes you to test every fiber of your being. For just as love is warm and tender, so it has a cold, hard quality that empties the heart of everything that is not Him.

The path of love is a journey into the unknown, into the darkness and wonder that lie within us. We are drawn into the bottomless depths of our own being, into a state of vulnerability and nakedness that for most people is too terrifying to consider. The poet Hâfiz writes: "The dark night, the fear of waves, the terrifying whirlpool, how can they know of our state, those who go lightly along the shore?" But Sufis are love's fools, His own personal idiots who do not care for their own safety, only for the eternal embrace of their Beloved.

This book is an attempt to share something of this path, of its beauty and terror, intimacy and awe. When Mrs. Tweedie was with Bhai Sahib in India, in answer to her many questions he would often reply, "You will know, by and by." She found that for the Western mind it is very difficult to be left continually in a state of un-knowing, and, when she returned to England, said that she would try to explain as much as possible. Many aspects of the path cannot be explained, because they belong to the inner recesses of the heart which cannot be grasped by the mind. Yet the mind can also play its part, helping us to understand the strange and often paradoxical ways of love. Spiritual life is so simple, because God is a simple essence. And there are ways to become attuned to this inner essence, to learn to listen and allow Him into our life. The ways of love flow according to their own rhythms, which are buried deep within us, often very different from the surface values of our life. Listening to the stories of the heart, we can become familiar with the deeper music of our own nature, and catch the thread of an inner unfolding that leads us beyond the limitations of our surface self, to something both wonderful and intoxicating. This ancient path of love is eternally alive, singing the mysteries of the heart, and since the beginning of time His lovers have been offering a taste of its wine that burns like fire.

2. THE ELEMENTS OF THE PATH

He travels with whoever looks for Him, and having taken the seeker by the hand, He arouses him to go in search of himself.

al-Ansârî

THE TURNING OF THE HEART

The path of love is alive and it takes us on the soul's journey Home. This is a journey of love to love, our own inner voyage into the unknown, to the further shores of the heart. Mystics are lovers going Home, living the passion and commitment that are needed to surrender and be taken, to become empty of oneself and filled with the Beloved. Little can be told of the innermost mysteries of the heart, of how our own soul opens to God. And for each of us this journey, our heart's pilgrimage, is unique, because we are unique. We are each a unique creation by the Great Artist, and each of us makes our own offering in the fire of love. But there are stages on this journey, doorways through which every pilgrim must enter, landscapes of the soul we all must pass through.

For many wayfarers the path begins with longing. One great Sufi said, "Sufism was at first heartache. Only later it became something to talk about." The soul's longing for God is the most potent anguish, the most primal pain. Just as love is the essence of the path, so is longing its agent of transformation. With one glance into our heart, with one sip of love's wine, He awakens our need for Him, the homesickness of the soul. And so we are taken into the arena of the heart's longing for God.

Many seekers first experience this longing as a discontent, what Saint Augustine called "the divine discontent." Without our knowing why, nothing in life seems quite satisfying. Life is no longer fulfilling. My teacher was happily married and she remembered one morning, before her husband awoke, having a cup of coffee and looking out through her kitchen window at the trees, hearing the early morning birds. She thought to herself, "I have everything I want, and yet it is not enough. Why?" At the time she just dismissed it as being her Russian temperament (she was of Cossack descent). Years later she came to realize the true nature of this feeling, how it was a foretaste of the path, of the intensity of the soul's hunger for what is Real.

We all come from God, but when we are born into this world we forget. We forget from where we have come and that we are children of light. We take on the clothing of this world, leaving behind the "clouds of glory" of our true Home. The Sufi calls this the "journey from God," a journey of forgetfulness in which we leave Paradise behind. But there are those who never quite forget, who keep a distant memory buried deep within them. As a result this world never seems like home; there is often a sense of not quite belonging, not fitting in. Mystics are strangers in this world, just because they remember their real Home.

The spiritual journey begins when this latent memory is awakened. For some people this is a gradual awakening that brings with it a sense of dissatisfaction. Your job, your friends, your relationship are no longer quite enough, and yet you don't know where to turn.

For some unknown reason life no longer answers your needs, but you don't know why. Maybe you take a vacation, try a new career, decide it is a "mid-life crisis." But the dissatisfaction remains. Then possibly something prompts you to begin to look for a spiritual path, find a deeper meaning to life, search for a teacher. The ancient journey of the soul has begun, a stage that the Sufis call *tauba*, the turning of the heart. This is when the journey from God becomes the journey to God.

For others this moment of *tauba* is more instantaneous, as when Rûmî met Shams. I remember for myself it happened one morning on the London tube train, when I was sixteen. I was reading a book on Zen Buddhism and came across the saying, "The wild geese do not intend to cast their reflection. The water has no mind to receive their image." This saying was like a key that opened a door within myself that I did not know existed. I felt a joy that I had never before experienced, a moment of intense exhilaration. For weeks afterwards I inwardly laughed and laughed, as if I saw the secret joke within creation. A world that had been grey began to sparkle and dance. I started to meditate and have experiences. Although it would be three years before I would meet my path in the outer world, my journey Home had begun. Years later I discovered that this saying about wild geese was a favorite of Bhai Sahib, Irina Tweedie's Sufi master. Asked to describe his Sufi path he would point to the birds flying across the sky, saying, "Can you trace the path of their flight?"

The moment of *tauba* is the awakening of divine remembrance. Sometimes people brush it aside; the last thing they want is to be distracted from their outer goals, their achievements, and to be taken into the vulnerability and need that are within them. But if the soul wants to go Home it will awaken you to its need, and however much you resist or try to distract yourself, this need will remain, never again allowing outer life to satisfy you. And under the surface is this longing, this pain of separation, because the heart has been awakened to the knowledge that somewhere, before the beginning of time, you were one with your Beloved. This is the poison that the Sufis often refer to, the poison of love-longing. You can try to push it aside, but the heart carries the power of love, the potency of our own connection to God.

Sometimes this moment of *tauba* will come in a dream, haunting, beautiful, mysterious; sometimes it will come straightforwardly and directly, as when a friend who was involved in politics heard a voice saying, "When are you going to stop playing around and do what you came here to do?" Listening to her dream, she turned her attention towards spiritual life. But this invisible thread is not always so easy to follow, because it is so different from the values of our outer life. Our material culture has so little understanding of the ways of the soul, and often the soul's dissatisfaction can be misinterpreted as a depression. In this extrovert Western culture we can feel a pressure to look in the outer world for a remedy, a new relationship or a new car, not recognizing the cry of the soul, a cry muffled by the noise of the world, hidden underneath our personality and our ego, deeper than our psychological problems.

THE FEMININE SIDE OF LOVE

Everything that comes into life has two sides, a masculine and feminine quality, even love. The masculine side of love is "I love you." Longing is the feminine side of love: "I am waiting for you. I am longing for you." Longing is the cup waiting to be filled. And sadly, because our culture has devalued the feminine, we have repressed so much of her nature, so many of her qualities. Instead we live primarily masculine values; we are goal-oriented, competitive, driven. Masculine values even dominate our spiritual quest; we seek to be better, to improve ourself, to get somewhere. We have forgotten the feminine qualities of waiting, listening, being empty. We have dismissed the deep need of the soul, our longing, the feminine side of love.

But the Sufi has always known that it is our longing that will take us Home, as Rûmî simply expressed: "Don't look for water, be thirsty." Rûmî knew the importance of longing, of having this inner thirst for God. Longing is the direct connection of the soul with its source, the link of love that runs between the Creator and His creation. Yet to acknowledge this need is very difficult for many people because it involves a state of vulnerability, and we are conditioned against being vulnerable. Longing awakens us to our own need, a need which we can never satisfy, and so we become infinitely vulnerable, exposed to this need. And longing also carries the pain of separation, the primal pain of the soul separated from the source. So why should we embrace our longing, live this sorrow?

One Sufi prayed "Give me the pain of love, the pain of love, and I will pay any price you ask. Give the joy of love to others. For me the pain of love." He knew the power of longing, how longing opens and purifies the heart and infuses us with divine remembrance. Longing is the heart's remembrance, the heart's consciousness of separation. Longing will take us into the arena of love, a love that will burn and transform us, empty us of ourself until all that remains is our Beloved.

Spiritual life is a giving of oneself to this need for God. He ignites the fire of longing within the heart, and our work is to let it burn. We can try to deny our longing, to run away—"I fled him down the nights and down the days, I fled him down the arches of the years"—to escape our own heart. Or we can give ourself to this primal pain, to the soul's need. We can become the wood for the fire of His love. We can honor the depth of His longing to be reunited with Himself within our own heart.

To live the heart's longing for God awakens us to our state of separation. Longing is the pain of separation, the pain that is underneath every other pain. And with this pain comes the awareness of Him from whom we are separate. Longing is the heart's remembrance of God, and as we live this longing, so we remember our Beloved. Longing turns us back towards God, and our tears wash away the veils of forgetfulness.

Remembrance is one of the most basic Sufi practices. With His glance He awakens our heart with the memory of union, and the work of the mystic is to bring this memory into consciousness. The path is a means to help us remember God, until one day our heart does not allow us to forget and in our consciousness He is always present, for He has said, "I am the companion of he who remembers Me." The mystic seeks to remember Him each moment of the day, with each and every breath. This does not happen on the level of the mind, because we live in the world and are involved with everyday activities. Sufism is not a monastic or ascetic path. But one of the mysteries of the path is the awakening of the consciousness of the heart, as is so beautifully expressed in the *Song of Songs*: "I sleep but my heart waketh; it is the voice of my beloved that knocketh, saying, Open to me my sister, my love, my dove, my undefiled" (5:2). When the heart is awake we are always attentive to our Beloved, waiting for His call.

The moment of *tauba* is the turning of the heart that awakens the lover to her Beloved. Longing brings into consciousness our need for His touch, for His embrace. Longing draws us from separation back to union. And the practices of the Sufi path are to keep us attuned with the energy of love, to help us to live this longing and come closer to our awakened heart, while it is the job of the Sufi teacher to keep this fire burning within the heart. Once a woman came to my teacher and said, "Look, I have this terrible pain in my heart, and I came to you hoping that it would go away." And my teacher said nothing because she knew that it was her job to keep this fire of love burning within the woman, to keep her awakened to her heart's remembrance of God.

The essence of the path of love is so simple and yet so easily overlooked. The heart wants to go Home; the heart cries for God. As Rûmî says, "I will cry to Thee and cry to Thee and cry to Thee, until the milk of Thy kindness boils up." When Irina Tweedie went to India to be with her teacher she took a small blue handkerchief. When she came back from India years later she kept the handkerchief as a memento, a handkerchief that was now white, bleached with all the tears she had cried. Anyone who has felt the pain of longing knows the reality of these tears, of the heart that "cries to God secretly in the night."

Our tears will take us Home. Giving ourself to our longing, we open the door of the heart to this crazy love affair with an invisible beloved. Sufis are lovers and madmen, prepared to gamble everything on this heartache. Because once you open the door of the heart your life will never be the same. You leave behind

the safety of the known world and set out into the darkness, the unknown, the passion and the madness of
love. If you give yourself to a human love affair you
may become a little unbalanced. Maybe you forget
things, are no longer punctual. When you are in love
you can behave in unusual ways, your values change,
and of course you suffer. How much more dangerous
is a love affair with God, a love affair that involves your
whole self, and does not carry the safety of being able
to isolate yourself from another person. Because this
Beloved is within your own heart, "closer to you than
yourself to yourself."

If this love affair is within the heart, why do I call
the Beloved He? God cannot be limited, is neither He
nor She. God has a tremendous, awe-inspiring masculine side as well as an infinitely beautiful, mysterious
feminine nature. God is the Absolute, but how can one
talk about having a love affair with the Absolute, or
with an It? As a human being I need to make this love
affair part of my human tapestry, because it is so real,
such an intimate unfolding. But there is another reason
why I call God He, which has to do with the nature of
the soul. The soul is feminine before God, waiting in
a state of surrender for the Beloved to come. The six-
teenth-century Indian princess and poet Mirabai knew
this mystical truth. Mirabai was devoted to Krishna, her
"Dark Lord," and once, when she was wandering in
some woodlands sacred to Krishna, a famous theolo-
gian and ascetic named Jiv Gosvami denied her access
to one of her Dark Lord's temples because she was a
woman. Mirabai shamed him with the words: *"Are not
all souls female before God?"* Jiv Gosvami bowed his
head and led her into the temple.

The lover waits for her Beloved. And when He
comes to us, in those moments of meeting and merging

that are so intimate that one can hardly speak of them, the lover is feminine, pierced, penetrated by the tremendous bliss of His love. He softens the tissues of our heart and shares with us the passion and the tenderness known only to lovers. He knows the ways of love, the intimacies of the heart's unfolding. Sometimes He seduces us with an inner touch, or He pleads with us to be with Him. For some it is suffering that opens us; for others kind caresses melt away our defenses. Often pain is followed by our yielding to His embrace, or we are awakened to a passion that can itself be frightening because it is beyond our control. With this inner lover there are no boundaries, nor the safety of separation. There is only the surrender of the soul to something so enticing that it can be terrifying, something so vast and endless that we are lost beyond any limits.

THE *DHIKR*

He awakens us to our longing, infusing us with divine remembrance. The work of the path is to help the wayfarer stay aligned to this power as it works within us, help us to give ourself to our heart's devotion. Every Sufi path has different practices, given by the masters of the path. The whirling dervishes turn in remembrance of their Lord; other Sufis chant their devotion, or have prayers that open the heart and align them with love. A central Sufi practice is the *dhikr*, the repetition of a name of God, or a sacred phrase. Repeating His name, we remember Him, and in the words of Kabir, "The breath that does not repeat the name of God is a wasted breath."

According to tradition there are ninety-nine names of God, but foremost among these is the name Allâh.

One great Sufi, Abû Saʿîd ibn Abîʾl-Khayr, had his heart opened when he heard the saying from the Qurʾan, "Say Allâh! then leave them to amuse themselves in their folly." And when he tried to study Sufism from books, his sheikh told him, "Abû Saʿîd! All the hundred-and-twenty-four-thousand prophets were sent to preach one word. They bade the people say 'Allâh!' and devote themselves to Him." According to an esoteric Sufi tradition, the word Allâh is composed of the article, *al*, and *lâh*, one of the interpretations of which is "nothing." Thus the actual word Allâh means "the Nothing." For the Sufi the fact that His greatest name means "the Nothing" has great significance, because Truth, or God, is experienced as the Nothingness (the same as the Void in Buddhism). And one of the mysteries of the path is that this Emptiness, this Nothingness, loves you. It loves you with such intimacy and tenderness and infinite understanding. It loves you from the very inside of your heart, from the core of your own being. It is not separate from you. Sufis are lovers and the Nothingness is the Greatest Beloved in whose embrace the lover completely disappears.

Repeating His name, in each moment we are making a remembrance of the nothingness of God, of His essential non-being. The mystic is making the journey from form to formlessness, from being to non-being, to the emptiness that underlies creation, what the Christian mystic the Blessed John Ruysbroeck calls "the dark silence in which all lovers lose themselves."

What is important about the *dhikr* is that it is performed with the breath. Repeating His name, we begin on the out-breath, "*al*," and then continue with "*lâh*" on the in-breath. At the beginning it can be difficult to begin with an out-breath; we often habitually begin the breath cycle with an in-breath. But there is a reason for beginning with the out-breath. Breathing out we empty ourself, and breathing in we then fill our whole being with His presence. There is also another, more esoteric reason. At the end of every in-breath the soul returns to its own plane of existence; without this the soul could not bear to be encased in a physical body. This is why, for example, when somebody dies his last breath is always an in-breath (often a last gasp); then the soul returns to its own plane and doesn't come back into the physical body. So with each breath we repeat His name, Allâh, and we return into the nothingness of God. With each breath we journey from the outer world into His presence within the heart, to the beyond of the beyond.

Repeating His name, we return to Him, and each moment is a precious affirmation of His presence. Many Sufi orders practice a vocal *dhikr*, chanting His name in a powerful and intoxicating evocation. The Naqshbandis practice a silent *dhikr*, reflecting a Qur'anic verse (7:55), "Call upon your Lord in supplication and hiddenness." Whatever our outer activities we strive to inwardly repeat His name continually. I remember when I was first given the *dhikr*. At that time this practice had not been made public, but was given individually. And I was so happy—I had been given a means to help re-member Him, whatever I was doing, wherever I was. No moment need be wasted; waiting for a bus I could repeat His name, lying awake at night I could say the name of the one I loved. Whenever I wanted I could turn my attention inward and continue my spiritual practice. One might think that to repeat the same word over and over again would become boring. If that is how you feel, then you will forget, then it is not for you. But if you love someone, you always want to think of him; your beloved's name is always on your lips. One of the mysterious qualities of love is that it does not belong to time, but to the eternal present. Repeating

His name is always for the first time, and each moment is an opportunity.

The *dhikr* is a simple but very powerful practice. Of course at the beginning you cannot repeat it continually. When the mind is occupied, talking, reading, or otherwise engaged, His name is not present. But whenever there is an opportunity, particularly when walking or performing physical tasks, then continue this practice. If while cooking you repeat the *dhikr*, the food has a special taste. The love in the food my teacher cooked was sometimes astonishing. I never knew that you could *taste* love until then. The *dhikr* makes simple tasks holy. Everything is an opportunity to remember Him. And the *dhikr* has a magic; it is said, "First you do the *dhikr* and then it does you." It goes into the unconscious and repeats itself within your heart. Then, even when your mind is busy with other things, if you look into your heart you will find His name is being repeated. You wake up and you are inwardly repeating His name. You may discover that even in your dreams you are practicing the *dhikr*.

The *dhikr* works in a number of ways. It helps to train the mind, so that we can become masters of our own mind. Normally the mind thinks us and not the other way around. Watch your thoughts and you will see how your mind leads you, even creating desires for you. Spiritual life is a process of becoming one-pointed, of focusing yourself on the Beloved. Repeating His name is a simple and highly effective way to control your mind and turn your attention back to God. It is said, "What you think so you become." For centuries lovers have used the name of their Beloved to help them realize their true nature, to make the journey from separation to union. By turning us away from the world and turning us back to God, His name holds us and aligns us with His grace and power.

The *dhikr* also works in the unconscious, purifying the psyche. This is a very mysterious process, but the power of His name works within the psyche, transforming us, as expressed in the *hadîth*, "There is a polish for everything that takes away rust, and the polish for the heart is the invocation of Allâh." Polishing the heart is a Sufi term for "inner work," for it is said that when the heart is free of blemishes then it reflects the pure light of the Beloved. Inner work is a very important stage on the path.

MEDITATION

The *dhikr* helps us to discipline and focus the mind during our everyday activities. But the spiritual path requires the complete stilling of the mind, and for this meditation is necessary. In order to have real spiritual experiences we need to stop the thinking process, for it is the mind that cuts us off from love's oneness and the infinite ocean of nothingness. Going beyond the mind, we enter the inner dimension of the heart, the meeting place of lover and Beloved.

Different paths use different meditation practices, each method a way of stilling the mind, for, as the American mystic Joe Miller expresses in his straightforward manner: "If you don't shut off the thoughts that you have running wild in your mind, you can't meditate and you can't be at peace with yourself." My teacher's path uses the energy of love to still the mind. Rather than attempting to still one's thoughts by focusing on the mind, through focusing on the heart and the feeling of love within the heart one leaves the mind behind. Thought-forms slowly die and our emotions are also stilled. The "meditation of the heart" is a practice that drowns the mind and the emotions in love. In this meditation, which should be practiced at least half an hour a day, we imagine three things:

1. We must suppose that we go deep within ourselves, deeper and deeper into our most hidden self. There in our innermost being, in the very core of ourselves, we will find a place where there is peace, stillness, and, above all, love.

God is Love, says the Sufi. Human beings are all love, for they are made in His image; only they have forgotten it long ago. When we love another human being, however deeply, there is a place in our heart where this beloved human has no access. There, we are quite alone. But within us there is a longing, which is the ultimate proof that this place is reserved for Him alone.

2. After having found this place, we must imagine that we are seated there, immersed into, surrounded by, the Love of God. We are in deepest peace. We are loved; we are sheltered; we are secure. All of us is there, physical body and all; nothing is outside, not even a fingertip, not even the tiniest hair. Our whole being is contained within the Love of God.

3. As we sit there, happy, serene in His Presence, thoughts will intrude into our mind— what we did the day before, what we have to do tomorrow. Memories float by, images appear before the mind's eye.

We have to imagine that we are getting hold
of every thought, every image and feeling, and
drowning it, merging it into the feeling of love.

Every feeling, especially the feeling of love,
is much more dynamic than the thinking
process, so if one does this practice well, with
the utmost concentration, all thoughts will
disappear. Nothing will remain. The mind will
be empty.

When we become familiar with this meditation we
no longer need to use the imagination. We just fill the
heart with the feeling of love and then drown any
thoughts in the heart. Emptying the mind, we create an
inner space where we can become aware of the presence of the Beloved. He is always within us, but the
mind, the emotions, and the outer world veil us from
Him. He is the silent emptiness, and in order to experience Him we need to become silent. In meditation we
give ourself back to Him, returning from the world of
forms to the formless Truth of the heart.

Drowning the mind in the heart, we offer to Him
our own consciousness, that spark of His Divine Consciousness which is His gift to humanity. So many wonders and so many evils have been enacted with His gift
of consciousness. But to make the journey back to God
we need to return this gift, this source of our illusion of
autonomy. Each time we go into meditation we sacrifice
our individual consciousness on the altar of love. In so
doing we give space for Him to reveal Himself:

Go you, sweep out the dwelling-room of your
heart, prepare it to be the abode and home of
the Beloved: when you go out He will come in.

Within you, when you are free from self, He
will show His Beauty.

Through love we still the thinking process and
give ourself to the infinite emptiness that is beyond the
mind. Of course it takes time to be able to still the mind,
to drown in love. This is the practice of a lifetime, but
gradually, day by day, year by year, the mind learns to
be left behind. We become familiar with the emptiness
in which there are no thoughts; we drown gladly,
knowing that we are taken beyond ourself by love into
love. Necessarily there are times we can meditate well,
and times when the mind refuses to be stilled and
keeps us captive. But meditation practiced regularly is
a doorway into the beyond, through which we receive
the deep nourishment of another dimension.

Sometimes in meditation we may receive a hint or
other guidance, because when the mind is stilled we
have more direct access to the Self. But what is more
important is that for a certain time each day we focus
inwardly, we make ourself available to what is beyond
this world. Once the mind is left behind, an instant is
the same as an hour, because time belongs to the level
of the mind. But it is deeply refreshing for half an hour
or more every day to put aside every thought or con-
cern, and allow His infinite emptiness, His limitless
nature, to take you where It will. Retreating from the
world and from oneself as a daily practice becomes
more and more important as one tries to live in the
presence of one's Beloved while being involved in
everyday life.

PSYCHOLOGY AND DREAMWORK

When Irina Tweedie went to India to study with a Sufi master, she said, "I hoped to get instructions in yoga, expected wonderful teachings. But what the teacher did was mainly to force me to face the darkness within myself, and it almost killed me." Every wayfarer has to face the darkness within, what Carl Jung called "confronting the shadow." Unless you face your own darkness you cannot purify yourself, you cannot create a clear inner space for your Higher Self to be born into consciousness. Jung said, "One does not become enlightened by imagining figures of light, but by making the darkness conscious." Then he humorously added, "The latter process, however, is disagreeable and therefore not popular."

Every path has its own methods for inner purification. The *dhikr* works in the unconscious, bringing the power of His name into the darkness. The meditation of the heart not only takes us beyond the mind, it also has the powerful effect of energizing the psyche and bringing our darkness to the surface. Like soapy water bringing the grime to the surface, meditation brings our darkness out of the unconscious. Anger, bitterness, resentment, jealousy, all the shadow feelings that we like to keep hidden, come up within us, forcing us to confront and accept them.

The Naqshbandi path has always stressed the importance of psychological work, and many of the initial challenges faced by the wayfarer involve accepting and loving her own rejected self, and doing battle with the *nafs*, the Sufi term for our lower nature. However, one of the difficulties of using traditional Sufi terminology for inner work is that the Eastern psyche is structured differently from ours in the West. For example, people in

India are much closer to the collective, the family is much more central to their lives, while in the West we have a more developed individuality. This is the immense value of Jungian psychology. Carl Jung gave us a model of psychological transformation that is based upon the Western psyche. He understood the processes of inner transformation that happen on the spiritual journey, and expressed these processes in a contemporary terminology.

When my teacher went to India she had studied Jungian psychology and was amazed to find that her teacher's process of spiritual training had similarities to Jung's process of individuation, although Bhai Sahib knew nothing of Western psychology. When she returned to the West she incorporated a Jungian model of psychological transformation to help the wayfarer understand the work of "polishing the heart." "Confronting the shadow" is the first step on the psycho-spiritual journey, followed by making a relationship with one's inner partner, the animus or anima in Jungian terminology, and then entering the archetypal realm, the world of the gods and goddesses. This psychological map leads us further, into the dimension of the Self, "that boundless power, source of every power, that lives within the heart." But finally psychology and Sufism part, because psychology aims at living a balanced life in this world, while the mystic leaves behind the ego, becoming lost in love's infinite oneness.

Sufis have also always valued dreams, and are often guided by dreams. Bahâ ad-dîn Naqshband, the founder of our order, was renowned as an interpreter of dreams. Our path integrates dreamwork within a spiritual context, and at our meetings we meditate, drink tea (an important time of just being together with other wayfarers), and share dreams. Just by our sharing a dream with an open heart its message can be heard. Dreams come from the unknown. Sometimes they retell the images of our daily life or lead us down confused corridors. But some dreams speak with the voice of the soul. They have a quality, a music, a depth of feeling that belong to the sacred part of ourself. Such dreams open "a little hidden door in the innermost and most secret recesses of our soul."

Listening to these dreams, we can hear the voice of our deeper self. Speaking to us in its own language, a language of images, symbols, and feelings, a dream can guide us through the tortuous maze of our psyche. As both teacher and guide, these dreams are of infinite value on the inner journey. They call us inward into the mystery and wonder that is our real nature. When the body is asleep, when our everyday life has laid down its burdens, these dreams tell us of another world and of a winding pathway that can lead us into the depths.

Sharing dreams, we all share in this mystery, and it doesn't always matter if a dream is understood consciously, because there is a deeper understanding of the soul. The soul of the listener hears the soul of the dreamer speak through the dream. Learning to listen to dreams, we attune ourself to the mystery of what is hidden within us, to the stories of our deeper self. Sufis listen with the ear of the heart, a heart that is open and receptive not just to the words that are spoken, but to the feelings and energy that come from the dreamer. With the ear of the heart we learn to catch the thread that is the guidance of the dream, the way the dream can lead us through the maze of ourself into the beyond.

Listening to ourself we come to understand more fully the complexities and simplicity of our nature. And within the shifting images of our dreams we catch the deeper meaning of our life's journey, the pattern of our life seen from the perspective of the soul, not the limited horizon of the ego. Dreamwork practiced within a spiritual context reawakens our inner perception, our ability to follow our inner path amidst the distractions of the outer world. Our own dreams and the stories of others tell the tale of the soul going Home, of finding the treasure hidden within us. Dreams guide us and teach us to catch the signs of our outer life and inner nature. They are the oracles of today, our own inner wisdom speaking to us.

THE RELATIONSHIP WITH THE TEACHER

Meditation, the *dhikr*, the remembrance of God, psychological work, and listening to dreams—these are all important tools to purify the wayfarer and take her Home. Another important element of the Sufi path is the relationship with the teacher. Sadly the relationship of teacher and disciple is often misunderstood in the West, causing much pain and confusion. In our Western tradition we do not have a model for the relationship with a spiritual teacher; it is not a part of our cultural context, as for example it is in India. Also in the West we have a tendency to personalize every relationship, illustrated by the way, in America, we tend to address everyone by his first name. Furthermore, the closer we feel, the more love we feel for someone, the more personal we want to make this relationship. The relationship with the teacher is both intimate and impersonal. These two qualities can appear irreconcilable opposites, until we realize that this relationship belongs *to the level of the soul, not the personality.*

The Sufi says that you need a teacher, you need a guide. In the words of Rûmî, "Whoever travels without a guide needs two hundred years for a two-day journey." The teacher is like a ferryman to take you from the world of the ego to the dimension of the Self, and as the Sufi Abû Sa'îd simply stated, "It is easier to drag along a mountain by a hair than to emerge from the ego by oneself." The teacher knows the inner potential of the student and helps her to grow into it, to make the journey to the farther shores of love. The teacher also knows the pitfalls and dangers of the journey, and if it is difficult to cross an unknown land or desert by oneself, it is far more dangerous to journey into the depths within oneself without a guide.

In the Sufi tradition, the teacher is traditionally "without a face and without a name," because it is the teaching that matters, the guidance and not the guide. However, for many wayfarers the difficulty arises due to the importance and intimacy of this relationship. For the sincere seeker the teacher is the most important person in her life: without her teacher she would remain stranded within her ego. At the beginning the wayfarer cannot recognize how this relationship belongs to the soul— that it is the soul that is guided, the soul that makes the journey Home. The wayfarer sees the teacher through the eyes of the ego, and through a conditioning that understands close relationships only as belonging to the personal sphere, as parents, siblings, friends, lovers. Moreover, because the relationship with the teacher happens within the heart, it carries a quality of intimacy and unconditional love that can be almost overwhelming. Thus the wayfarer only too easily projects onto the teacher all of the personal patterns that have been attached to parent-figures or lovers. Only much later, usually after a painful process of detachment (often accompanied by dreams of the teacher dying), does she come to recognize the real nature of this relationship. After I had been with my teacher for a few years I was told this truth in a dream: "You can only possess the teacher when she turns into a basket of bread and wine."

What if you don't have a teacher? How do you find a teacher? Once again the spiritual reality is quite different from our preconceptions. You don't find a teacher, the teacher finds you. Through our aspiration and inner work we brighten the light within us, and when this light is strong enough it will attract the attention of a teacher. It may appear outwardly that we read a book or hear about a teacher, but spiritual processes always begin on the inner planes and then manifest on the physical. One friend had a dream in which she was in a green English field, in love with a white-haired woman. She awoke from the dream and the feeling of being in love remained. It seemed crazy, to be living in New York and to be totally in love with a figure in an English field in a dream. Then one day she was in a book shop and a book literally fell off the shelf; picking it up she saw the face of this woman on the cover. She flew to England where the woman lived, sat in her meditation group and cried and cried tears of love and longing. She had found her teacher, after her teacher first found her through a dream.

The teacher opens our heart to love and gives us the sustenance we need for the journey. My teacher used to say that coming to meditation meetings was like "recharging the batteries." The teacher also always points us inward, to the real teacher which is the light within our own heart. The end of the spiritual training is when we can be guided from within, from our Higher Self within the heart. The Sufi also says that the greatest teacher is life. Sufis believe that we attract to ourself the circumstances we need to learn from. One of the differences between the ordinary, worldly person and the seeker is that the seeker is not so interested in outer success or failure, but looks to see what a situation has to teach him. He asks himself, "Why did I attract this situation and what do I have to learn from it?"

Sufism is not an ascetic or monastic path. Sufis marry, have children, follow a trade or profession, and at the same time keep the inner attention on the path. Abû Sa'îd expressed this very simply: "The true mystic goes in and out amongst the people and eats and sleeps with them and buys and sells in the market and marries and takes part in social intercourse, and never forgets God for a single moment." It is not easy to be involved in the outer life and yet remain true to our inner goal. There are so many distractions, particularly in our very materialistic Western culture. Naqshbandis try to practice the principle of "solitude in the crowd": "In all your outer activities remain inwardly detached, learn not to identify with anything whatsoever." We engage in the outer world, following our everyday life as a nurse, or lawyer, or car-park attendant, but do not identify with our external role or activity. For the Sufi external roles are of small, relative importance. What matters is that within the heart we look towards our Beloved. In this world we are His servant, playing the role that has been given to us, but for the lover all that matters is his Beloved. Sufis are known as slaves of the One and servants of the many. In our daily life we help in the world, but within the heart we remain His slave.

However, it is not always easy "living in the two worlds." Meditation may open your heart to another reality, but you have to keep your feet on the ground. A few years after I met my teacher I had an important dream, in which I was invited into the presence of Bhai

Sahib's teacher, and he showed me a film of himself as a young man flying a kite. The message of the dream was simple: if you want to fly high you have to keep your feet on the ground. I knew that this was something I would have to learn because in my early twenties my feet were definitely not on the ground. I had had some mystical experiences and often found everyday life quite confusing. But through family life and my work as a schoolteacher I learnt to keep my feet on the earth. Everyday difficulties are a great help, balancing the limitless inner dimension with the constrictions of outer life.

Joe Miller said that there are four qualities necessary for spiritual life. The first is common sense, the second is common sense, the third is sense of humor. When he was asked what is the fourth quality, he replied laughing, "Even more common sense!"

In a Sufi group there is always much laughter, a laughter that is never unkind but knows the frailty of being human. There is a famous Sufi trickster figure, Mulla Nasrudin. One day a friend walked by and saw Nasrudin searching in the dust in front of his house.

> "What are you looking for?" the friend asked.
>
> "I've lost my keys," replied Nasrudin.
>
> So his friend kindly stepped over the fence and helped Nasrudin to look for his keys. But after a while, when the keys had not been found, he asked, "Nasrudin, where did you lose your keys?"
>
> "I lost them inside my house."
>
> "But why are you searching out here then?"
>
> "Because there is more light than inside."

So often we look for the key of our life, for what will give us meaning, outside of ourself. We look with the harsh light of rational consciousness. But the Sufis have always known the secret that the key is within our own heart. The path of love gives us access to this key, which opens the door of the heart, the door that separates us from our Beloved. Once we step through this doorway into the arena of His love for us, love takes us. Love seduces us, leading us along the most ancient pathways of the soul. We are drawn into the intoxicating states of nearness and then seemingly abandoned in the states of separation. The completeness of this love overwhelms us and our need increases. We are caught in love's trap, awakened to the depth of our longing. Working on ourself, practicing remembrance and meditation, we clear an inner space for our meeting. Then He draws us to Him. Silently, unexpectedly, our Beloved comes to us and dissolves the veils of separation. The experiences of the soul are so intimate they can hardly be spoken, but we come to know that we are loved completely and absolutely. We have come back to the place where we belong, to the dwelling place of our desires.

3. THE ONE THING

There is one thing in the world which you must never forget.

Rûmî

THE DESTINY OF THE HEART

The call of the heart awakens us. We are drawn onto the path, drawn into the circle of love, into the mystery of our innermost nature. But what are the qualities we need to make this journey, to travel from the world of separation into the oneness that is found within the heart? For the lover the whole path is contained within love: the path is love. The journey of our soul is to live this love, the deepest love that exists, the connection between the Creator and His creation. This is our primal purpose as mystics, as wayfarers. In the words of Rûmî, this is the "one thing in the world which you must never forget":

> There is one thing in the world which you must never forget. If you were to forget everything else and remembered this, then you would have nothing at all to worry about; but if you were to remember everything else and then forget this, you would have done nothing with your life.
>
> It is as if a king sent you to a country to carry out a particular mission. You go to that country, you do a hundred different things; but if you do

not perform the mission assigned to you, it is as if you have done nothing. All human beings come into the world for a particular mission, and that mission is our singular purpose. If we do not enact it, we have done nothing....

Now if you were to say, "Look, even if I have not performed this mission I have, after all, performed a hundred others," that would mean nothing. You were not created for those other missions. It is as if you were to buy a sword of priceless Indian steel such as one usually finds only in the treasuries of emperors, and were to turn it into a butcher's knife for cutting up rotten meat, saying, "Look, I'm not letting this sword stay unused, I am putting it to a thousand highly useful purposes." Or it is as though you were to take a golden bowl and cook turnips in it, while for just one grain of that gold you could purchase hundreds of pots.

Or it is as though you were to take a dagger of the most finely-wrought and tempered steel and use it as a nail to hang a broken pitcher on, saying, "I'm making excellent use of my dagger. I'm hanging a broken pitcher on it, after all." When you can hang a picture on a nail that costs only a few cents, what sense does it make to use a dagger worth a fortune?

Remember the deep root of your being, the presence of your lord. Give your life to the one who already owns your breath and your moments. If you don't, you will be exactly like the man who takes his precious dagger and hammers it into his kitchen wall for a peg to hold his broken pitcher.

You are more valuable than both heaven
  and earth.
What else can I say? You don't know
  your own worth.
Do not sell yourself at a ridiculous price,
You who are so valuable in God's eyes.

We come into this world in order to love Him. For the Sufi this is our deepest destiny which is stamped within the heart in fire. We bring this purpose with us into the world, and when our heart is awakened we feel this need of the heart, this call of the soul. If we give ourself to the heart's need, then we are fulfilling ourself as human beings; we are doing "the one thing needful." Everything else is secondary. Only this innermost destiny has real purpose.

Yet, as Rûmî says, it is so easy to forget this "singular purpose," to do a hundred different things and avoid this call of the soul. We so easily get distracted, caught up in inessentials. We think of all the things we have to do and avoid the one thing we *need* to do, the one thing that we came here to do. It is as if you go into a supermarket to buy a loaf of bread, but end up looking at the shelves and putting into your basket many different items, and only when you get to the check-out do you realize that you have forgotten the bread. Our world is like a supermarket, full of so many distractions, some of which seem very meaningful, but which do not carry the primal purpose of the remembrance of God. When Mary sat at the feet of Christ, she was criticized by her sister Martha, who was so busy about the house. Yet Christ praised Mary above the busy Martha:

> Martha, Martha, thou art careful and troubled
> about many things:
> But one thing is needful: and Mary has chosen
> that good part, which shall not be taken away
> from her. (*St. Luke* 10:41–42)

So easily we busy ourself, engage ourself in activities, and overlook the "one thing needful." We forget.

THE DEEP ROOT OF OUR BEING

The purpose of the path is to keep us focused, turning us away from all the inessentials that so easily consume us. The path awakens the remembrance of the heart and, despite all of the distractions, keeps our attention on this mystery that unfolds within us. Each of us has our own particular distractions, ones that are most powerful in diverting us. There can be outer desires—for a bigger house, a better job—but it is often our inner needs that are more powerful. For some this may be the desire to be useful, or to do good, while others may have a powerful unlived need that clamors for attention, for example the need to be emotionally supported, or to be appreciated, or even the need to be a victim. Shadow qualities are often as powerful an attraction as more seemingly fulfilling needs.

One of the difficulties of living the "one thing" is that then so much appears to remain unfulfilled, to be unrecognized. Many aspects of ourself that we may feel to be important have to be left by the wayside. This can evoke feelings of betrayal, as we may have to sacrifice what seems an important need, perhaps a pull for recognition, even a creative drive. We are each unique and carry a unique combination of qualities, many of which may have to be discarded, and they can complain with the cries of abandoned children. But always there is the deeper pull towards the heart's real purpose, towards a oneness that eventually will include all aspects of ourself. Christ's saying, "Seek ye first the kingdom of God, and his righteousness; and all these things shall be added unto you" (*St. Matthew* 6:33), speaks of an inclusion that is born from a one-pointed search for Truth. Giving ourself to God is an offering to our own innermost nature, to our own true being. In this essential being all aspects of our real self are included. What is excluded, what is left behind, are attributes that do not really belong to us, the baggage we have picked up from our childhood or family patterns. But only later do we realize this.

"Remember the deep root of your being." If we remember this quality that we carry within us we will return to our essential nature, and thus be able to make our own unique contribution to life. Our roots are fundamental to our existence, but they belong in the darkness of the inner world. Hidden deep beneath the surface of our life, they are almost invisible, often only appearing in dreams and visions. The inward nature of "the deep root of your being" makes it so easily overlooked, especially in our extrovert Western world where the outer, tangible aspects of our existence dominate consciousness. In our daily life, when we are bombarded by so many outer images, caught in so many sensations, how can we recognize our essential nature? If this quality is not reflected by our environment, how will we come to know it?

In previous times and other cultures the inner world was given greater value; the symbolic, mythical dimension of ourself was given prominence. The wayfarer living amidst the complexities and chaos of our present culture has to rediscover this inner dimension. She has to find the "priceless sword," the "golden bowl" of her true self and learn to use it for the purpose for which it was designed. She has to bring it into the arena of her life and allow it to transform her, to take her Home.

In the moment of the heart's awakening we are given a glimpse of our innermost nature. But this glimpse is then clouded, lost amidst the impressions of our daily life. When we come to the path our outer life rarely echoes our true self, but rather carries the baggage of our conditioning, the superficial values of our materialistic culture. In order not to lose our most precious thread we need an environment where it is reflected back to us, where the deeper self is given prominence. Here lies the importance of a spiritual group, a place where the values of the soul are primary. A spiritual group carries a focus on the "one thing we must never forget" and this creates an atmosphere in which we can recognize this quality within ourself. The group reflects back to us our own spiritual nature, reminds us of our "deepest mission."

In a Sufi group the energy of remembrance, meditation, and devotion creates an invisible light in which the wayfarer can see more clearly the purpose of her soul. In this sacred space the world of the personality and ego, which dominate our outer life, is put aside, and for a few brief hours each week we are immersed in a different atmosphere, in a deeper belonging. Here we can catch the thread of our soul's destiny and slowly bring it into our daily life. In the light of the group's remembrance we can recognize the potency of our own remembrance, feel the power of our soul's need. We can begin to step out of the world of the ego into the dimension of the Self.

A Sufi group belongs to the invisible world where the heart sings the remembrance of God. Meditating or just being together, we become immersed in this inner song. The weary traveler steps into the circle of the friends of God and is given the nourishment she needs to continue the journey. She is reminded of her own longing, of the call of the heart. She is drawn back to the hidden center of herself.

LIVING WITHOUT RULES

A spiritual group reflects back to us our deepest self. But then we have to recognize this quality, to own it and to live it. We have to take responsibility for what the world rejects, and not misuse our "priceless sword," our "golden bowl." Belonging to the inner world of the soul, it is easily dismissed, its value overlooked. It is "the stone which the builders rejected, is become the head stone of the corner" (*Psalm* 118:22). One of the difficulties at the beginning is that this inner quality, this "particular mission," is very different from everything we know. The "golden bowl" does not belong to the limited container of our everyday life, a life defined by personal patterns and collective values. It belongs to the infinite part of our nature, to the limitless horizons of the Self. And it carries the potency of real freedom, of which we are often afraid. We easily talk about freedom, but this is usually the freedom of the ego to do what it wants. Real freedom takes us beyond the bounds of our limited self, beyond the cozy walls of our conditioning. Real freedom means never knowing what is going to happen, and never resisting change. For many people freedom is just too terrifying.

Sadly, as Rûmî says, we often use our golden bowl to cook turnips. How does this happen? For example, one wayfarer has an inner devotional nature that longs to serve God. But she grew up in an environment in which spiritual service was unrecognized, and so her devotional nature was caught in family patterns in which the woman serves the man. And so she adopted this outer service, attracting men who demanded her subservience. Thus her true devotional nature remained unlived, until the path found her and she began to discover this inner orientation in which she could live her need to serve the divine.

Many women are unknowingly caught in a collective conditioning in which the feminine is made subservient to masculine, rational values. The feminine qualities of relating, listening, waiting are repressed in favor of rational thought and goal-oriented drives. American culture may appear to give freedom to women, but there is a collective pattern that denies the real nature of the feminine. As one woman said to me, "In this culture a woman can be anything she wants, as long as it is masculine." Yet many spiritual qualities needed for the path, such as creating a sacred inner space, belong to the feminine. Often our spiritual nature lies buried under collective taboos, and requires courage and commitment to be rediscovered and lived. Using our golden bowl for the purpose for which it was made is never easy.

Finding and living our inner freedom comes at a price. The wayfarer has to face the patterns of the collective, the sense of being rejected, and even the fear of persecution. We carry ancestral memories of being persecuted for spiritual truth, and the mystic has often been ostracized or punished for seeking direct inner revelation. Marguerite Porete, a Beguine Christian mystic, was burned at the stake in Paris in 1310. Her condemnation

is not surprising when we read some of the radical words
she wrote describing her mystical ascent:

> The soul at the highest stage of her perfection
> and nearest the dark night is beyond noticing
> the rules of the Church. She is commanded by
> pure love, which is a higher mistress than what
> we call "charitable works."
> ... If anyone were to ask of such free souls ...
> if they would wish to be in paradise, they would
> say no. Besides with what would they wish it?
> They have no will at all, and if they were to wish
> for anything, that would mean severing them-
> selves from Love.... For that one all alone is my
> God of whom one cannot utter a single word,
> of whom all those in paradise cannot attain a
> single atom, no matter how much knowledge
> they have of Him.

Living one's innermost nature is a state of pure love,
a love that does not belong to the conventions or regulations of this world. In the words of Rûmî, "Lovers have
a sect and religion all of their own." This freedom is
undefined and unrestricted because it belongs to the
undefined and unrestricted part of our self. It does not
mean *doing what you want* but *being who you are.*
For the mystic this means living one's innermost connection to God.

Learning to live without definition or restriction is
not easy. For the mystic there is no visible set of rules to
follow, no prescribed patterns or imposed order. I was
once told this very clearly in a dream: "You cannot walk
the path of straight with rules." The path is too straight,
too one-pointed to be defined by rules, because rules
by their very nature are limiting, and the path to the

infinite has to be unlimited. What is right for one person is wrong for someone else. Some people have to learn to be poor, while others need to take the responsibility of having money. Some wayfarers have to learn to love, while others need to discover the vulnerability of being loved. Each in our own way we are taken by God to God, according to His ways; and His ways are often the opposite of what we think is spiritual. The great Sufi Dhû'l-Nûn expressed this very simply: "Whatever you think, God is the opposite of that."

However, although the path is too free to be defined by rules, the Sufi has to live by the highest ethics. On our path we are taught that to have something you do not use is like stealing; even keeping an overdue library book is stealing. One should also try never to hurt another's feelings. The Sufis call the ethics required for the path "chivalry." We stress generosity, having a good nature, refraining from passing judgment on one's fellow men. We do not impose our beliefs upon others, because "we respect the variety of human paths, beliefs, opinions, and ways of conduct," and "we believe that all paths lead to the Beloved." Also "we try to give precedence to our friends over ourselves; yet we use our honest discrimination so as not to abuse our self-respect."

But these principles of the path are only guidelines, because what is more important is that we learn to follow the hint, the guidance that is given within the heart. This guidance belongs to the moment, not to any defined set of principles. In the West we are conditioned to define and plan our life, to follow the course set by our goals and outer objectives. But if you follow your heart you have to give yourself to a path that promises insecurity, vulnerability, and an openness to the unexpected. You have to learn to read between the lines of life, to catch the subtle hints that are given by both the inner and outer world, for in the words of the Qur'an (Sûra 41:53), "We will show them Our signs on the horizons and in themselves."

Catching the hint that is given, we live the mystery that calls us, not deviating from the single purpose that draws us Home. This mystery is His imprint within the heart. When someone comes to a Sufi group for the first time, he or she is often asked, "Why have you come?" This question has tremendous significance for it brings into consciousness the soul's purpose, the heart's imprint. The wayfarer has to find out why he came and then live this answer, live it with the passion and determination that are demanded by the path.

We have to discover what really matters to us, what is the most important thing in our whole life, and then have the courage to live this deepest dream. Carl Jung said, "Find the meaning and make the meaning your goal." Whatever is most meaningful should be our purpose, whether this is to be a successful businessman or to climb a mountain. But if this one thing is to realize the Truth, then you are a mystic. And to follow the path of a mystic takes courage because you are doing something which does not belong to the mind or to the senses, but to the unknown and the unknowable. As the Sufi Inayat Khan said, "It is like shooting arrows in the dark, you see the bow and the arrow, but you don't see the target."

THE PRICE OF A KISS

The mystic focuses on the one thing needful, even if it means ignoring the hundred other things that are clamoring for attention. What this means in daily life is that we focus on the remembrance of the heart while we conduct our everyday affairs. We are responsible men and women and take our place in society, whether as doctors or carpenters, but we also live the consciousness of our connection with God. What is ignored, or left behind, are many of the unnecessary distractions that consume so much time and attention. If you look closely at your activities and thought-patterns and sincerely ask, "Are they helpful? Do they make a real contribution to my life?" you will find that many of these patterns are just ego-driven and benefit no one.

Spiritual discrimination is learning where to use your energy. We each have a certain amount of energy, and we need this energy to fulfill our daily life and go to God. Yet sadly, most people scatter themselves in a thousand unnecessary directions, and so do not fulfill their deepest purpose. Spiritual life is learning to become one-pointed, to harness one's energy for the sake of the path. The practices of the path, meditation, the *dhikr,* and inner work, help us to become more one-pointed, to be able to focus our energy rather than being dragged by the mind and our psychological patterns in many contrary directions. But we also need to use discrimination, to learn what activities to engage in—for example when to help others and when it is better to leave them alone. Slowly we free our energy from the grip of the patterns of the ego and the *nafs* or lower self, and use it to be responsible in our daily life and to fulfill the heart's calling.

The cruelty of the path comes from what has to be left behind, what has to be discarded. We discover that many patterns that appeared so important are just attachments that stand in our way. Some of these may be outer material objects. But it is usually easier to deal with outer attachments—for example, sell a car—than to discard psychological attachments—the need to be liked, for example, or the desire to be helpful. But these patterns block our energy, hold us imprisoned. Rûmî says, "Do not sell yourself at a ridiculous price, you who are so valuable in God's eyes." And yet through these patterns we sell ourself again and again. We sell ourself for all sorts of different reasons, for emotional support, to be accepted—some reasons are obvious and some more hidden.

Sometimes we sell ourself just to avoid doing the "one thing needful." We busy ourself with so many useful things, good causes or negative patterns, just to avoid knowing our true worth. Because once we realize that we are "so valuable in God's eyes," then we have to take responsibility for our own true value and can no longer live as victims of life, no longer hide from our self. We are taken into the arena of our own self where we have to stand naked before our Lord and accept the dignity and beauty of being His servant.

We are so valuable in His eyes because we carry the remembrance of Him, His stamp within our heart. We carry the memory of the kiss of our Beloved. And His love calls us to live this kiss, a kiss that is more precious than our own self. Rûmî describes the potency and price of this kiss,

> I would love to kiss you.
> *And the price of kissing is your life.*
>
> Now my love is running towards my life
>   shouting,
> *What a bargain, let's buy it.*

The price is to give everything, even our self, for the kiss of our Beloved. This is a lover's commitment and it is given gladly because we know the wonder of His touch, the intoxicating beauty of His presence. Although we have to leave behind so many attachments, so many things that the world says matter, we give it freely despite the pain that may be caused. He seduces us into His presence. The Indian mystic Tagore tells a moving story:

> A Yogi was telling his beads by the Ganges when a Brahmin in rags came to him and said, "Help me, I am poor!"
>
> "My alms-bowl is all that is my own," said the Yogi. "I have given away everything I had."
>
> "But my lord Shiva came to me in my dreams," said the Brahmin, "and counselled me to come to you."
>
> The Yogi suddenly remembered he had picked up a stone without price among the pebbles on the river-bank, and thinking that someone might need it hid it in the sands.
>
> He pointed the spot to the Brahmin, who wondering dug up the stone.
>
> The Brahmin sat on the earth and mused alone till the sun went down behind the trees, and cowherds went home with their cattle. Then he rose and came slowly to the Yogi and said, "Master, give me the least fraction of the wealth that disdains all the wealth of the world."
>
> And he threw the precious stone into the water.

The secrets of the heart are infinitely precious and they are given freely by the Beloved to those who love Him. They are free because the Beloved is free; "they are given, as a gift." And yet we have to pay. This is one of the paradoxes of the path. We pay with our devotion, with our longing, with our sacrifice and surrender. We pay with the pain of being emptied of everything that separates us from our Beloved, because "two cannot live in one heart"; we must choose either the ego or the Beloved.

Through our connection with the Beloved we bring His presence into our life; we live according to His invisible ways and not our own patterns and desires. At the beginning the path seems so intangible, so easily lost, but then slowly the path grips you; it runs through your heart like a thread of finest steel, yet is as soft as a rainbow, a rainbow full of eternal promise. Through this connection, this path of love, the currents of His love for us flow faster and faster, stronger and stronger. This love is the power that melts away our defenses, burns up our ego, transforms our lower nature. This love makes us so vulnerable, so naked, until all that remains is the soul's cry for God.

Why is this tender, burning love so terrible, why does it demand such a price? Because it knows no limits, will not be fenced in. This love belongs to the great Beloved, not to some buying and selling of affection which we term love. And this love wants to be known within the heart of the lover, so it has to clear away the obstacles that stand in its way. This is the painful process of purification, the longing that aches and burns. Day by day, week by week, year after year, His love works within our heart and psyche, even in the cells of the body, purifying, clearing away the rubbish we have accumulated. The Sufis call this "polishing the mirror of the heart." It may appear to be work upon the shadow, upon one's negativity and bad habits, but really it is the work of love. We learn to become soft and tender and yet as hard as tempered steel. We are emptied and transformed, and the price is everything we think precious, everything that seems to matter except the "one thing."

LIVING THE ONENESS OF LOVE

There is a Sufi saying, "Keep away, keep away from the lane of love." Why should His lovers advise others to keep away from the road that leads back to Him? Because they know the demands of the journey. Rûmî describes how this path is not for "brittle, easily-broken, glass-bottle people":

> A self-sacrificing way,
> but also a warrior's way, and not
> for brittle, easily-broken, glass-bottle people.
>
> The soul is tested here by sheer terror,
> as a sieve sifts and separates
> genuine from fake.
>
> And this road is full of footprints!
> Companions have come before.
> They are your ladder.
> Use them!

Others have come before and left their bloodied footprints as reminders of the price of love's kiss, the price of living the call of the heart. To dare to live the oneness of love requires courage and a little craziness; one gambles one's life, one's sense of self, on this invisible love affair. Why should we make this journey of remembrance when so many live in forgetfulness? Why should we challenge the conventions of the world when so many people are content with what the world has to offer? Why should we be so reckless? Because, as Rûmî says, if we do not we have done nothing with our life.

Love enacts a strange revenge. She offers so much: ecstasy, fulfillment, a tenderness beyond any human touch. But if we open to love and then withdraw we are left with the deep sorrow of a life unlived, a grief for something that was never done. That is why it is better never to start than to start and draw back. And this is the burden of free will. We have the choice to say "Yes!" to the burning demands of His love, or to say "No, not now, not yet." And our Beloved respects our choice, because He gave us the gift of free will. But once we have tasted just a sip of the wine of divine remembrance, the wine that was before the creation of the vine, then we can never entirely forget. There is a strange poison that remains, a sense of a journey we could have made.

But if you say "yes" to love, say "yes" with the passion known only to lovers, you give youself to a mystery that takes you into the beyond. You say "yes" to a life without boundaries, and learn to live on the borders of the unknown. This is the secret known to the Sufis, the secret of the heart, the hidden oneness of love. Because when He loves you it is with an intimacy that other lovers can only dream of. Every human love affair belongs to duality: you and your beloved are two separate people. However close, however intimate, the relationship remains on the level of duality, with all the problems of loving someone who is different from you. But mystical love belongs to oneness. He *is* your heart, your most intimate self. Nothing can compare with this love affair, with the totality of His embrace. What human lovers long for, mystics live.

But the path takes you to the edge of yourself, to the deepest patterns of your insecurities and to the vulnerability of your wounds. To be open to love is no sweet romance, but a burning intensity that demands everything. The cry of the soul is always with us, but there are reasons that we avoid it, that we try a thousand things rather than this "one thing." There are the reasons of common sense and self-protection that make us turn away from the lane of love. These are reasons that the path is "not for brittle, easily-broken, glass-bottle people." But lovers belong "to a deeper season than reason," which is why Sufis are known as "idiots of God." We are His own personal idiots because we give ourself to what we can never grasp, can never understand, can only wonder at. We stand with the golden bowl of ourself in our hands and say "Do with me as Thou will."

The real mysteries of the path can never be put into words, because they belong to a different dimension, a reality that the mind cannot grasp. But there are the footprints of this path, the tales told by lovers. Sufis love to laugh and tell stories, like the story of the minister who comes to the gates of heaven, where Saint Peter is waiting. Saint Peter looks down his list of those who can go to paradise, and tells the minister that he is not on the list. The minister starts to complain, saying how he has been a good minister, how he belongs in heaven, how he has studied the scriptures and looked after his congregation. As he stands there arguing with Saint Peter a local bus driver who has just died arrives, and Saint Peter, glancing at his list, waves him straight on through the Pearly Gates. The minister is astonished and indignant. "He was just a bus driver. I was a minister, preaching the word of God to the people." "Ah," says Saint Peter, "but while you were preaching many people were sleeping. While he was driving everyone was praying!"

This is the path of the Sufi, the wild ride on the bus, always on the edge of the inner abyss, like the buses in the Himalayas, where you look out of the window at the river flowing through the rocks, thousands of feet below, and the bus turning the corner sends stones over the edge, crashing into the chasm. On this journey there is neither safety nor security, just the intensity of your own devotion to hold you. All you can do is pray, but this journey keeps you awake, helps you to remember why you are here. The path of love keeps ignited the fire of the heart, the fire that is His love for us. The mystic lives this fire, burns with the longing of divine remembrance, the longing that will take her Home.

And this wild ride of devotion happens in the midst of everyday life, of going to work, having a family. It is a mystery that happens within the heart, a journey for which there is no visible path. We search for our Beloved and our Beloved searches for us; "light upon light, Allâh guides to His light whom He will." In the closed circle of His love for us there is only the heart merging into the heart, love being absorbed by love. The Sufi path is a way to live this loving, to remember the deep root of our being and give our life to "the one who already owns our breath." A friend recently wrote to me:

> I discover more and more that in my life I have so much: beautiful children, a wonderful work, friends around me—but everything is nothing if the One Thing is missing, if He is not with me, if my heart is dead.

4. THE JOURNEY HOME

No one by himself
can find the Path to Him
Whoever goes to His street
goes with His feet.

Maghribî

THE INNER LIGHT THAT GUIDES US

Sufis believe in dreams, in the wisdom and guidance that come to us in the night when the mind is asleep. Some dreams are a window into the inner world, through which we can glimpse the path of the soul, experience the wonder of our infinite self. These dreams tell stories, tales of the heart's journey. They speak to us in the symbolic language of the psyche, the ancient language of the soul that has been sadly overlooked and forgotten in our rational world. Listening to these dreams, we are given insight into the workings of the psyche, the way the path unfolds within the life of the dreamer.

The following dream was dreamed by a ten-year-old girl who grew up in a small village in Yorkshire; she told me this dream when she was in her late twenties. She said that in her village when she was a child there was no electricity. The Yorkshire moors where she lived have a wild beauty, and can also be very bleak and cold. "And what used to happen," she said, "was that when you had someone coming to visit you in the evening, you put a lantern in the window, and you opened the door so that the light would shine out and the visitor would see where to come. In the dream, it's evening and I am coming home to this cottage where I live. But first I have to cross a road in which shadowy figures are passing back and forth."

This child's dream tells in simple imagery the whole spiritual path. The spiritual path is a journey home, back to where we really belong. That is why people so often experience a feeling of sadness in their lives, the feeling that something in their life is missing, the feeling that they want to be somewhere else. Because deep down inside they are feeling the homesickness of the soul, what the Sufis call longing. Mystics are travelers, wayfarers on the journey to our real home, as is echoed in a saying of the Prophet, "Be in this world as if you are a traveler, a passer-by, because this is not home. Sometimes you sit under the shade of a tree, sometimes you sit by a lake, with your clothes and your shoes full of dust, but you are always a passer-by because this is not home." This dream describes the journey home in the simplest imagery: the girl is going home and there is a light to guide her through the darkness. Inside her, in the house of her real self, there is a light shining through the open door. And this light is what beckons her across the darkness; this light is what brings her home.

The simple wisdom of a child tells of the light in our own heart that shines to us through the darkness of the world. And the spiritual path is just a journey back to ourself. This light is within all of us, though for some it seems to shine more brightly than for others, for some it is more visible. For this ten-year-old girl, her light was already beckoning her, though it would be a number of years before she consciously stepped upon the path, picked up the thread of the journey that this dream imaged. Each in our own way, we come to the path, and yet this journey is eternally present within us, because it does not belong to time or the realities of the mind, but to the dimension of the soul.

We have to make the journey back to ourself, to the light that beckons, and yet paradoxically we are never separate. The greatest journey does not lead anywhere, because we are already at home within ourself. Recently I asked a seeker what was her goal, to which she replied, "To find my true self." But how can we lose our true self, how can we need to find what we already are? This is one of the greatest contradictions of the path: we have to find what we already are, to journey back to ourself, "to the root of the root" of our own being. And this journey that seems to evolve through time, through years of searching and struggle, is like a fully formed embryo within us, waiting to be lived. This is why dreams can be so precious, because they come from the part of us that *is the journey* and *knows where we are going*. Often when we first come to the path we are given a dream that outlines the whole journey, the essence of the struggles and joys that we will encounter. We know the way home, and yet we have to search so hard to find it.

This ten-year-old girl knew the way home, knew the light that would guide her through the open door of her own self. In her dream she also knew the obstacles she would confront, the "shadowy figures crossing back and forth." With the eternal wisdom of a child she knew of the darkness that she would find within herself, the shadow aspects that stood between her and her inner light. The journey to the light is made through the darkness of the unconscious, of what is repressed within our psyche, the fears, pain, and shadowy aspects of our self that every seeker must confront and accept. Only through accepting our own darkness can we discover the light of the Self. When the eleventh-century Sufi al-Ansârî was asked the secret of contentment, he replied, "When one has learned with love to accept."

INNER WORK AND THE GROUP

All spiritual paths are just an elaboration on the same theme: we want to go home; we are homesick for our real self. We are called back to ourself, and our light guides us. Rûmî begins his most famous poem, the *Mathnawî*, with the lament of the reed torn from its bed. In these lines one can hear the wailing sound of the reed flute, the Sufi *ney*, whose haunting call echoes the longing of the heart:

> Listen to the reed how it tells a tale, complaining
> of separations,
> Saying, "Ever since I was parted from the reed-
> bed, my lament has caused man and woman
> to moan.
> It is only to a bosom torn by severance that I can
> unfold the pain of love-desire.
> Everyone who is left far from his source wishes
> back the time when he was united with it."

The heart calls us to go home, awakening us to knowledge of separation. Before, we were asleep, blissfully ignorant of our true nature. But now love stirs us from our sleep, shows us what we have lost, and urges us to find it. Yet if we did not know our real home we would not look for it, we would not know that we were separate. The very fact that we are making this journey, facing our darkness and our fears, means that within us we know where we belong, somewhere that is not here, not in this world, and yet is not anywhere else.

Our longing calls to us through the darkness, pulls on the thin thread of our devotion. And our dreams will often outline the way, show us the work that needs to be done. For each of us this journey is our own unique inner unfolding, and our dreams image this uniqueness, speaking to us in the language of our own soul. For some the path is a descent to the underworld, for others a climb up a mountain. Some dreamers find a child in their arms whose eyes have the light of stars, while others meet mad drunkards who demand all their money and identification. This young girl saw the path in the powerful imagery of her own village life, in which the soul's magic is present, and also the fear of the unknown, the shadowy figures who cross in front of her.

Many seekers are put off by the idea of confronting their darkness. We like to imagine spiritual life as sweetness, kindness, the loving parent we never had. Our own darkness is like a guardian of the threshold, separating those who have the courage and conviction to make this journey from those who are spiritual window-shoppers, or seekers looking for a "quick fix." Once I was giving a dream workshop and a woman asked me why she never dreamed. I said, "Maybe you are so balanced and so much in touch with your inner nature that you don't need to dream?" "No," she honestly replied. "Then maybe you don't want to deal with what your dreams will tell you?" She protested that she wanted to know what her dreams could reveal. "Well then, are you prepared to spend the next three to five years discovering what an unpleasant person you are?" I will always admire the honesty with which she replied, "Oh no!"

Our shadow contains the secret of our transformation. It is the lead that will be turned into gold. But the process of "polishing the mirror of the heart" is hard, warrior's work, requiring honesty, integrity, and courage. As W. B. Yeats remarked, "Why should we honour those who die on the field of battle? A man may show as reckless a courage in entering into the abyss of himself." And the Christian poet Gerard Manley Hopkins expresses the same feeling in the lines,

> I am gall. I am heartburn. God's most deep decree
> Bitter would have me taste; my taste was me.

Working on the shadow takes commitment, time, and energy, and often there seems to be very little change, just the uncovering of more problems, deeper pain, more intense feelings of isolation, rejection, abandonment—whatever are the feelings hidden behind the doors of the unconscious. One friend was really astonished, saying that she had read about the conflicts and struggles of the path, but never expected work on the shadow to be so real, so intense. Cruelty, jealousy, anger, resentment, bitterness, and other shadow qualities may surface without warning. Seeking a greater wholeness, we are confronted with the opposites of what we think we are and what we discover we are. Trying to reconcile these opposites within us, we find ourself caught in conflicts painful and bitter. Outer arguments pale beside these inner struggles that can be violent and tormenting. And the greater the aspiration, the greater the devotion, the quicker the darkness comes to the surface.

This intense inner work demands much of our attention and energy, and yet we have to continue our everyday life, with all its outer demands. Added to the stress is the fact that we live in an extrovert culture that does not value inner work, and our friends and col leagues may be disturbed by the fact that we are no longer so outgoing or interested in surface activities. Here lies the value of a spiritual group, a community of friends who support and encourage your efforts. Usually this support is a silent inner confirmation of the importance of the inner journey, but it can also be helpful at times to share a little of the struggles and dramas that unfold. In our Sufi tradition we share and discuss dreams, and in this process offer a container and an understanding of the individual work of uncovering the darkness and polishing the mirror of the heart. This is a journey we all have to make alone; no one can do this work for us. And yet, as Rûmî writes,

> You may be happy enough going alone,
> but with others you'll get farther and faster.
>
> Someone who goes cheerfully by himself
> to the customs house to pay his traveler's tax
> will go even more lightheartedly
> when friends are with him.
>
> Every prophet sought out companions.
> A wall standing alone is useless,
> but put three or four walls together,
> and they'll support a roof and keep
> the grain dry and safe.

Bahâ ad-dîn Naqshband, after whom the Naqshbandi order is named, said, "Ours is a way of group discussion." A group provides a place where the inner journey can be shared and its deeper meaning understood. A group can give us the strength we need to walk alone through the maze of our own psychc. And what is central to a Sufi group is that it leaves us free. There are not the usual rules of belonging that structure many other groups. All that is required is a desire for Truth. A Sufi group is one of the few places where we are allowed to be ourselves, because Sufis believe that we are made in the image of God, and if a human being is set free she will find her own way back to God. Coming to a Sufi group is stepping into a circle of freedom that supports the inner integrity of the human being. And not everyone who comes to a Sufi group is a Sufi. Anyone who needs the nourishment offered by this circle of friends is welcome, as long as he does not disturb the group. The door is always open. A Sufi group does not belong to the rules and regulations of this world, with its barriers and discrimination, but to the Beloved; we come together for His sake. And a meditation group is always free—money cannot be charged for spiritual practices. Everything is given through the grace of God. So those who need, who are drawn to a Sufi group by the invisible thread of their soul's hunger, are given what they need. I will always remember talking to a young opera student from New Zealand, who came to our group in London for a little over a year. Her musical training in London was over and she had to return home, and she doubted that she would have the money to return in the near future. I asked her what her time here at the group had given her, and she replied, "I learned to let my song sing me and not the other way round."

People come for a day, a month, a year, or forever. Wounds are healed, dreams are discussed, and the inner work of the soul is given prominence. And always, underneath, in the silence, there is the ancient song of homesickness, the cry of separation, the reed torn from the reed-bed. This is the heart's cry for the Beloved, the longing that draws us home. In our outer life so much is conditioned; there is so much buying and selling. But in a Sufi group the wine of love is free; the only cost is to face our own darkness and become empty for His sake. Yet this is the ultimate price, the price of ourself.

THE HANDS THAT HELP US

The journey home takes us into our darkness where we discover our light, the light of the Self that guides us. This light is always here, always within us, pointing out the path through dreams and inner promptings, a silent unveiling of our journey in which we are able for a moment to see more clearly our direction. This light *is* the way, the path that is revealed, the guidance that is given. *Light upon light,* and yet it is only one light, the light of His love within our own heart.

And although a spiritual group is of immense value, the mystical path is always a solitary journey, from *the alone to the Alone.* We can only be guided by our own light, we can only journey within ourself, and for each of us this journey is different, an uncovering of our own unique essence. This is why the Sufi says that the outer teacher always points to the inner teacher, to the light of the Higher Self, and the end of the path is to be able to be guided by this light within our own heart. Surrendered to the Self, we live in the presence of God. This is when *the journey to God* becomes *the journey in God.*

Often on the path we feel the pain of this alone-ness. Even in the company of fellow wayfarers we experience a quality of solitariness that is deeper than loneliness because it does not belong to the personality or the ego. As we travel a path that takes us away from the comfort of the collective and its patterns of co-dependency, we feel the aloneness of the soul. My teacher used to say, "What have I to offer? I stand alone on the mountain, and look down into the valley where the sun is shining and people are playing, laughing, and crying. Here there is only a desolate emptiness with the wind howling, and yet I am close to God."

Alone we journey into the alone, solitary we embrace the solitude of the soul. And this inner, instinctual aloneness can often evoke the shadow of the collective and its social values that do not understand the mystic's deep need to be alone. We are an outcast from the collective patterns that offer a sense of security and belonging to so many.

The degree of aloneness that is required for this ultimate journey can be too terrifying for many people, and they should wisely stay away from the lane of love that empties the heart of everything. For the mystic the inner journey to the root of the root of their own self is everything, everything that matters, everything that has substance. We journey to the edge of the known and then further, leaving behind all traces of what we thought we were. The poet E. E. Cummings describes the strange wonder of this transition, and how we find a deeper connection to a love that is beyond ourself and yet is our own essence:

> losing through you what seemed myself,i find
> selves unimaginably mine;beyond
> sorrow's own joys and hoping's very fears
>
> yours is the light by which my spirit's born:
> yours is the darkness of my soul's return
> —you are my sun,my moon,and all my stars

Why do we make this strange journey? Because love calls us, love wants us for itself. Love draws us into the aloneness of our own nature, into the solitude of the soul. Love wants to share with us the mysteries of creation, the wonder of the link of love that runs through life. And it is said that when we make this journey, when we say "yes" to love's call, then all of creation helps us. Love's journey home is the greatest adventure, the supreme test, and is also the ultimate aim of creation. Every atom longs to return home; every atom sings the song of separation. And when a human being turns inward and is prepared to sacrifice herself on love's altar, then creation turns towards her. There are hidden lights that guide us, that come to meet us. So often it seems that we are left with our aloneness, but we are given so much help, so much grace. "If you walk towards Him, He comes to you running."

The moment you step upon the path, life works differently. The forces that govern your life begin to change. In the West we are very identified with the outer laws of cause and effect, with the importance of individual will and the hubris that has given human beings an all-powerful image. We have forgotten the simple fact that the world belongs to God. Turning towards Him, we align ourself with His power, and with the forces within creation that help the needy traveler.

The journey home is His journey back to Himself, and "Allâh guides to His light whom He will." This may go against all of our values of self-determination and equal opportunity, but the mystic follows a path that is determined by His will and not our ego-oriented consciousness. On this path the traveler is helped and protected by invisible forces, by unseen hands. Joseph Campbell's phrase "Follow your bliss" rings in the heart of every lover, but the words that follow are not so well-known, "and if you do unseen hands will open doors that you did not know existed."

These unseen hands come in many guises. We know of chance meetings that change our lives, the books that fall off the shelves into our hands. We are less familiar with the invisible forces that shape us, the gods who can be terrible and wondrous, the whole patterns of existence that lie concealed behind the visible world. Our culture's stress upon the rational, external world of the senses has cut us off from the inner dimension that was the foundation of past civilizations, and we are taught to disbelieve what we cannot touch or measure. Children often see their guardian angel, the watchful spirit that is appointed to every human being. But growing up we are conditioned to believe the world seen by our parents, and so we forget: "and down they forgot as up they grew."

Knowingly or unknowingly the wayfarer needs the help of the inner world to cross the mountains and deserts he encounters. It is not necessary to see or feel the forces that come to our aid, but we soon come to realize that we cannot make this journey alone. We have to be inwardly supported, to be guided through the maze of our self. In the Sufi tradition the teacher is the guide, and his presence is always with us. Bhai Sahib once humorously remarked, "What a trouble it is to be a guru. You have to be with all of the disciples all of the time." This help that carries us is given on the level of the soul, which does not know the limitations of time and space. Moreover, a great soul can be present in two or more places at the same time, in the same way that the rays of the sun fall on different places.

We are nourished by the grace that comes through our sheikh. In our moments of despair we are contained by the energy of the path and "the line of our spiritual superiors" to whom we are connected. Yet because most of this help happens on the inner planes beyond our consciousness we cannot attach to it our patterns of dependence or bargaining. Like the sunshine it is given freely.

I grew up in a spiritual group from when I was nineteen, and became used to miracles happening. There were the simple miracles, people healing more quickly than the doctors understood, or a friend having a baby when she had almost given up hope. And there were the deeper miracles of the heart opening, of love being created, of the life of a person changing. It happened within myself and I was privileged to see it happen to others: a wounded casualty of life learning to walk upright, sensing the beauty and power of his real nature. Slowly our attitude to life changes. Healed *from the center of our self*, we are given back our birthright, the joy and dignity of being human. And most miraculous, the light in the person's eyes changes; there is a sense of a wonder that cannot be put into words. This is always a gift; we know we cannot do it ourself.

EVERYTHING IS GIVEN

In our aloneness we are held, journeying from the isolation of our own ego to a sense of belonging, of being known for who we really are. On this path we have to make every effort, more effort than we ever believed possible, and yet everything is given. This is one of the most bewildering realizations: the paradox of the effortless path. You cannot reach the goal without effort, and yet your own effort will not take you even to the first waystation.

Here lies the mystery of surrender: we make every effort but finally we can only surrender. Only His arms can carry us over the threshold. One friend had this simply explained in a dream:

A man was lying on a bed crying because he wanted to grow up. One woman present said, "That means to become self-sufficient."

But a man who was also present said, "No, it means to surrender."

For so many years we struggle to stand on our own feet, to give up our patterns of dependency. This is a necessary part of our journey, to value our own self and to make our own contribution to life. But self-sufficiency belongs to the sphere of the ego. The dimension of the Self knows a deeper truth: that we are dependent upon Him. He is the light of our life and gives us all we need.

Stepping into the arena of the Self, we leave behind the values of the ego. We still need to stand upon our feet, be a responsible member of society, and yet we begin to realize the totality of our dependence upon our Beloved. Although we live in an outer world of separation, we glimpse a oneness that embraces everything, that underlies all of creation. And we come to know that we are a part of this oneness. We belong to Him whom we love, and because we regard life as determined by Him, we turn to Him in everything. There is an amusing story about the great eleventh-century Sufi Abû Saʿîd ibn Abîʾl-Khayr:

Abû Saʿîd was speaking before an assembly and he said,

"Today I am going to speak to you about astrology."

All the people listened to the Sheikh with keen interest, wondering what he would say.

The Sheikh said, "Oh people, this year whatever God wishes shall happen, just as last year everything that happened was what God, He is exalted, wished."

Living in the presence of God is a state of surrender to everything that is given, because the lover, having tasted the oneness of all life, knows that everything, whatever its appearance, is a gift from his Beloved.

The mystic is one who is not bound by appearances. He has journeyed from the unreality of the outer world to the reality that is found within the heart. The mystic knows that he cannot know God, who is "beyond even our idea of the beyond." And yet he is drawn into the circle of love's truth, into the oneness that underlies the multiplicity of life. Here he realizes the totality of his dependence upon his Beloved, how the circle of love and of all life belongs entirely to God.

Held in His invisible presence, drowning his individual consciousness in the ocean of the heart, the mystic merges into the emptiness that is deeper than any form. And in this emptiness he discovers his essential nature, "the face he had before he was born."

There is an essential part of us that is always with us, and we spend so many years looking for it. We search for it in books, in music, in love affairs. We follow this mysterious thread of our inner existence, sensing it in dreams, visions, moments of peace in nature. Sometimes at sunrise when the world is at peace we may feel this quality of something other which is so close to us; walking by the ocean we may be reminded of a different rhythm which we know and yet cannot grasp. This is our own self calling to us, leading us on our journey home.

A journey implies movement and progression. We search for Him with every effort until, weary and exhausted, we give up. We have to look, even though the object of our search never left us but is with us in our looking:

> I will search for the Friend with all my passion
> and all my energy, until I learn
> that I don't need to search.
> ...
> But that knowing depends
> on the time spent looking.

Driven by the instinct that somewhere He has to be found, we walk in the dust and heat of the road, laughed at by villagers who are sensible enough to stay at home. But of course there is nowhere to go, because He for whom we search is not separate from us. Our search leads us to the place of desperation until finally our heart breaks open to the emptiness where He is always present, to the timeless moment of love in which we are bonded together.

We need to search in order to find what was always within us, because only then do we know our real nature. Sufis tell a story about some fishes who made the great journey in order to find out what water is:

> There was a lake and in this lake there lived many fish. It was a beautiful lake. There was enough to eat, there were many trees around the lake. The sun shone almost every day because it was in the south. The water was not too cold and the fish were very, very happy.

But one day after a heavy rain in the hills, the river swelled and carried into the lake a trout.

"Ha," said the trout, "this is a lake and bigger than the river. But this lake is really a boring place."

So the trout swam around and looked at everything, and said, "Water is not flowing here. There is nothing that interests me to eat here. I want flies and there are no flies here. There are just a lot of silly little fish." And the trout jumped into the air and said, "I bet they don't even know what water is," and he swam back into the river.

The fish looked at each other and said, "What did he say? We don't know what water is? I wonder what he can mean!" And so they founded a university and had workshops and seminars and intellectual exercises, and invited wise fish. However, nobody was able to tell them what water is. So little by little they became depressed, and had conflicts and needed psychological healing. But none of it helped. Then one day someone remembered that far, far away, at the end of the seventh lake, there was a very wise fish. He was hundreds of years old. He was so mighty and wonderful that he was all white. So they decided to swim there and ask him what water is.

They swam through the first lake, where some were caught by eagles and others by fishermen. In the second lake more were caught, and others became too tired to go on while still others found tasty morsels and were diverted from the journey. So it went on until out of the hundreds who had started only thirty or forty arrived in the seventh lake. At the end of that lake there was a cave, and in that cave there was a very big, white fish. It was enormous and almost blind, and it was in *samadhi*. The little fishes all made a circle around him and waited.

Eventually the wise old fish opened his eyes, which twinkled, looked around him and said, "Brothers, why have you come here? What do you want?"

"Sir," one of them timidly asked, "we came to ask you a question."

"What is the question?" asked the fish.

"Sir, we want to know what is water."

The fish did not answer, but he closed his eyes and went back into *samadhi*. The little fish stayed there, patiently but with pumping hearts.

After a long while he opened his eyes, and said, "My friends, I do not know what water is. But I can tell you what water is not. Water is not the sky, water is not the clouds, it is not the grass, it is not stone, it is not the trees." And he talked for a very long time telling them what water is not. Then he closed his eyes and went back into *samadhi*.

So the fish looked at each other and said, "He told us what water is not. Ah! Maybe water is where we are!"

And they became very happy, and swam away back to their little lake and lived happily ever after.

5. TWO WINGS OF LOVE

God turns you from one feeling to another
and teaches by means of opposites,
so that you have two wings to fly,
not one.

Rûmî

THE MASCULINE AND THE FEMININE PATH

Everything that comes into life has a dual aspect, positive and negative, masculine and feminine. Even the primal energy of love has a masculine side, "I love you," and a feminine side, "I am longing for you. I am waiting for you." The spiritual journey itself also has a masculine and feminine nature. The masculine aspect of the path is to seek a goal, to seek union with God or Absolute Truth. This masculine dynamic gives us the focus and perseverance we need to make this journey, to travel beyond this outer world of illusion to the inner reality that lies within the heart. For the masculine, Truth, or God, is not here in the world around us, but in the beyond.

However, for the feminine He is always present. The feminine embraces the deepest secret of creation in which the Creator and His world are eternally united in love. The feminine knows that God *is* because she carries the mystery of life within her; she can give birth to life. The feminine knows that life cannot exist without this sacred substance, without this essence. This is the sacred nature of the feminine which our culture has sadly forgotten and is only now beginning to rediscover. For the feminine there is no journey, because in the wholeness of life everything is eternally present; the circle is always complete because the nature of the feminine is wholeness.

However, this wonder of wholeness, of divine oneness, is hidden within the feminine. It is a secret which she knows and yet has forgotten, just as many women have forgotten their own sacred nature. The instinctual feminine loves to keep her wisdom hidden because she fears the harsh light of consciousness. In the light of consciousness the mystery of life is so easily lost and this brings deep pain to the feminine. She knows how easily her sacred space is violated at the hands of masculine consciousness. To bring something into consciousness is to confront it with the opposites, and so break apart its sacred wholeness, destroy the feminine's instinctual knowledge of the oneness of life.

Consciousness confronts us with the opposites, which in the Garden of Eden are described as "the knowledge of good and evil." The natural wholeness of life does not know this duality, a duality which banished us from paradise. The feminine understands that if you make something conscious you can lose its wholeness, and so she instinctively prefers to remain hidden, to keep her knowledge concealed. Bringing her innermost understanding into consciousness confronts it with the limitations of time and space, with the sharp edges of analytic thought, with a linear, rational mind-set. And yet if she remains always hidden she never comes to consciously know her own divinity, her own sacred nature. The feminine path is to make conscious this inner wholeness, the instinctual link of love that unites the Creator and the creation. She has to accept the duality of consciousness and yet remain true to her innate knowing of wholeness. Her work is to bring the circle of love, the natural wholeness of the Self, from the instinctual world into consciousness.

The masculine path takes us away from the world of multiplicity into the oneness that lies beneath the veils of creation. The feminine always embraces this oneness because she is a part of the Great Mother who is the oneness of all life. But this knowledge is hidden within her, and, like all aspects of the Great Mother, carries the taboo of consciousness. The great flow of all life does not know its own oneness. Only humankind has the ability to make this oneness conscious, and yet consciousness carries the pain of separation, the eviction from the paradise of oneness.

Consciousness banished us from paradise, from the natural sense of being in which animals live. Yet consciousness also opens a doorway through which we can rediscover our true nature. If we can contain the contradictions of a society which so often denies our essential self, consciousness can help us rediscover what we appear to have lost. Within the heart all the contradictions are contained in a deeper love that gives us a knowing beyond duality. In this knowing the masculine and feminine aspects are united, and we come to discover that our natural self carries the secret of our divinity.

THE DUAL MOVEMENT OF THE SPIRAL

One of the difficulties confronting the contemporary wayfarer is that most texts describing the spiritual journey have been written by men and emphasize the masculine journey of renunciation. They stress the need to turn away from the world and seek a oneness that can only be found elsewhere. The ancient feminine mysteries embrace life and reveal its secret meaning. But these mysteries were rarely written down. In ancient Greece they were taught at Eleusis and for over a thousand years were the center of religious life, but it is a testament to their power that despite the thousands of initiates their secrets have never been made known. The feminine is naturally hidden and the secrets of creation do not show themselves easily.

The quality of the masculine is consciousness. While the feminine likes to remain hidden, the masculine seeks to make itself known. The masculine leaves its imprint only too visibly while the feminine is veiled. We live in a culture that values what is visible and easily rejects what is hidden, yet we know we need to embrace both. The masculine and feminine need to be united in our quest, for they are both a part of the spiral path that is our journey Home.

A spiral has both a circular and a linear movement. The masculine takes us in a linear direction, towards a goal, which can appear to be upward or downward but in truth is inward. This linear direction demands a focus of intent and a conscious commitment to persevere despite all the difficulties that may be encountered. The feminine is the spiral's circular movement, which is inclusive. The feminine requires us to be flexible and continually changing, responsive to the inner oscillations of the path. To remain fixed is to remain static, caught in a concept or form. The journey Home is a journey of freedom in which all concepts or ideologies are swept away. We need to allow ourself to change beyond recognition, to be swept into a dance that takes us beyond ourself. The Sufi Master

Bhai Sahib described where he lived as "a house of drunkards and a house of change."

There are times on the journey when we need the strength of our masculine commitment, when we need to be focused despite all the difficulties or temptations that may bombard us. And then there are periods when we need to be accepting and responsive, when we need to flow with the currents of change. The danger is always to remain caught in one aspect of the path, with one spiritual pattern or attitude. We need to recognize the masculine and feminine aspects of the journey within us, to discover our strengths and also our weaknesses, and to remember that sometimes a weakness can open a door which our strength leaves closed.

Men may find it easier to live the focus and perseverance demanded by the quest, while for a woman it can be more natural to embrace the receptive qualities needed to be attentive to the call. However, men and women have both masculine and feminine qualities and these are reflected in our spiritual drive. In each of us masculine and feminine are emphasized to a differing degree. There is also the collective conditioning that may overshadow our natural tendencies. For some women the masculine focus of the quest is easier than the all-embracing feminine; the ideal of renunciation is easier than the instinctual awareness of life's sacred nature. This masculine emphasis can be the result of cultural conditioning, a wounding of the feminine, or a deep orientation of the soul. Just as there are many variations across the physical spectrum of masculine and feminine, so is a wayfarer's orientation not limited to sexual type-casting. There are men who are in tune with the creative dance of life and can find the Beloved most easily in the mysterious beauty of His forms. An artist may have this spiritual temperament and through surrendering to his work come closer to Him whom he loves.

In the spiral dance of love we need to embrace both masculine and feminine qualities, to breathe in and to breathe out. Yet we also need to acknowledge our own nature, to find our own way of being with God. The Sufi Râbi'a was one of the great women saints and she stressed the supremacy of divine love, in contrast to some of the earlier Sufis who stressed asceticism. Yet she had a quality of inner focus that could not be disturbed. She could not be distracted by the forms of the world, as in the story of when, one glorious spring day, she was sitting inside with the shutters drawn. Her maid came to open them, saying "Look outside at the beauty the Creator has made." But she refused to step outside, and Rûmî tells one version of her response:

> The gardens and the fruits are in the heart—
> Only the reflection of His kindness is in this
>   water and clay.

Rûmî himself withdrew from the world when he met Shams-i Tabrîz. Divine love called him and he left his family and disciples, making them so jealous that in the end they chased Shams away. With Shams Rûmî traveled the road that leads far beyond the forms of this world:

> I was invisible awhile, I was dwelling with Him.
> I was in the Kingdom of "or nearer," I saw what
>   I have seen.
> ... I have gathered a wealth of roses in the
>   garden of Eternity,
> I am not of water nor fire, I am not of the
>   forward wind,

I am not of moulded clay: I have mocked them all.
O son, I am not Shams-i Tabrîz, I am the pure Light.
If thou seest me, beware! Tell not anyone what
    thou hast seen!

But Rûmî's capacious nature embraced both the
masculine and the feminine. In the same poem he also
describes a oneness with life in its differing aspects:

I am the pangs of the jealous, I am the pain of
    the sick.
I am both cloud and rain: I have rained on the
    meadows.

Unlike Râbi'a, Rûmî celebrates the beauty and wonder of the creation:

Thanks to the gaze of the sun, the soil became
    a tulip bed—
To sit at home is now a plague, a plague!

To deny the creation is to deny the link of love
that runs through all of life. Within the heart there is no
separation, no need to turn away from form, because
it embraces formlessness. Love is an ocean without
limits and the feminine includes everything within her
sacred arms.

INCLUSION AND EXCLUSION

Within the heart everything is one; the masculine and
feminine are united in love. The wayfarer needs to live
both aspects, to turn away from the world of illusion and
yet also embrace the wholeness of life. Looking within,

we find which qualities are easy and which need to be developed. Personally, I have always found renunciation easy; an inner focus on the path is an integral part of my nature. The challenge has been to embrace life in its multiplicity, to realize the wisdom of the feminine. Family life has been a wonderful teacher for me, as my children threw me into the chaos and beauty of the ordinary, forcing me to accept life with its contradictions, difficulties, and miracles. I could no longer turn away from the world, but had to realize life's sacred wholeness amidst the intensity of ordinary human experiences.

Feminine and masculine, inclusion and exclusion— we need both of these qualities: the wisdom of union and the wisdom of separation. On the path of love even renunciation is a limitation, as in the saying, "Renunciation of renunciation is renunciation." To be "in the world but not of the world" is to embrace the world with all of its confusions and glory, "the pangs of the jealous, the pain of the sick." When we open our heart to life we are not limited by duality or caught in contradictions, as I discovered to my own surprise. My family took me both into life and back to my Beloved. Suddenly in the midst of everyday activities I would feel His presence, see His face within His creation.

The heart is the home of the Self and the Self contains all the opposites within Its essential oneness. The multiplicity of life reflects an inner oneness; oneness makes itself known through multiplicity. To deny the wonder of multiplicity is to deny the life that enables us to recognize that He is One. We are not only a mirror to His beauty but a part of His beauty. We carry within ourself the hidden secret of creation, the secret that is brought into existence by the very word of creation, "Be!" (*"Kun!"*).

The feminine, caring for all of her children, knows the danger of exclusion. Life is sacred only in its entirety, only because *everything is He*. True renunciation is not the renunciation of the world but the renunciation of the ego, of one's limited, separate self. However, because the ego's identity is so embedded in the outer world, in possessions and attachments, turning away from the world can be a process of breaking the grip of the ego, freeing ourself from its patterns of identity. If our individual identity is contained in an outer position, in a beautiful house, or in the car we drive, we are imprisoned in these limitations. Struggling to look only towards Truth, to identify with what is highest within ourself, we need to cut these cords of attachment.

In turning away from the world, the wayfarer is turning from the ego towards the Self. The Self, "lesser than the least, greater than the greatest," is a quality of wholeness that contains everything, including all life, within itself. The Self cannot exclude anything, as reflected in the story of the soldier who asked Jâmî if he was a thief. The great saint replied, "What am I not?" Turning towards the Self, the wayfarer's personal self becomes included within the greater dimension of his innermost being: "whole, he passes into the Whole."

Renunciation is a falling away of attachments as the wayfarer is caught and held within the larger dimension of the Self. The lesser falls away under the influence of the greater. Each step we take on the path towards Truth increases the influence of the Self, whose energy has the effect of dissolving patterns of ego-attachments. The Self gives us the power we need to turn away from the world. Without this power we would be forever under the spell of the ego and its patterns of illusion. The ego is so strong and its attachments so potent that the wayfarer could never break its grip. Only because we are included within the greater dimension of the Self are we able to make the transition, to step into the spiral of the path.

At the root of renunciation is the journey from our own isolated self towards union. This journey demands that we leave behind the ego, that we "die before we die." We need to cooperate with the energy of wholeness that separates us from our own limited sense of self, our identity, our values and attachments. We need to see the limitations of our own life as we know it, its emptiness and illusory nature. And we need the sword of love to cut us away from our attachments, just as we need the warmth of love to melt the boundaries of our own being.

Contraction and expansion, in-breathing and out-breathing—the path is a continual process of movement and change. There are times when we need to focus and keep our attention one-pointed. But there are also periods of expansion when the heart opens to include a diversity of experiences, when the manifold aspects of both ourself and the Beloved come into consciousness. The real limitation is to remain caught in one stage, in the masculine dynamic of contraction or the feminine quality of expansion. Each has its time and purpose, and then changes into its opposite. The guidance of the Self and the energy of the path activate the movement of the spiral and the inner process that accompanies it. The danger is that we can remain attached to a particular spiritual dynamic. For each of us, different aspects of the path are easier and more appealing. Some wayfarers find the masculine energy of renunciation more attractive, while the feminine work of inclusion may evoke feelings of vulnerability. Others are naturally attuned to the work of embracing, and find the knife of exclusion difficult to wield.

DIFFERENT CHALLENGES FOR MEN AND WOMEN

The path presents different challenges to each of us,
different lessons and unlearnings. I had to free myself
from the drive to renounce, the desire to turn away from
the world. The path took me into the marketplace of
life, where, rather than losing God, I found a greater
completeness and deeper freedom. And yet, what held
me, in the midst of all this turbulence and the myriad of
impressions, was an inner focus on something beyond
this outer world of forms. As a man I needed to claim
this inner quality, to master my own nature while giving
myself to life.

We all have masculine and feminine qualities within
us, but men and women are made differently: physically, psychologically, and spiritually. Because a woman
creates new life from her own body she has an instinctual understanding of the spiritual essence of life. This
knowledge comes from the creative power of God which
she receives in her spiritual and psychic centers at birth.
A man has to work hard to gain this knowledge. A man
needs to transmute his instinctual power-drive until it
is surrendered to the will of God. A woman's instinctual
nature always connects her with the spiritual essence of
life, but man's instinctual drive has to be transformed in
order for him to realize its divine potential. In her natural
self a woman is always at the sacred center. A man has
to make his heroic journey in order to rediscover within
himself his spiritual nature.

Women instinctively know life's wholeness, but find
it difficult to leave outer attachments. Generally it is easier
for men to be detached and to focus on an invisible goal.
Irina Tweedie explains this:

> Because women have children they are
> made in such a way that things of this world
> are more important than for a man. We need
> warmth, we need security. For a woman a
> home, warmth, security, love, are very much
> more important than for a man. You will see
> in India many more male *sannyasins* than
> female *sannyasins*. For a woman it is much
> more difficult to renounce the world.... For
> us women spiritual life is easier than for
> men, but to renounce is more difficult than
> for men.

For a woman, detachment can carry the pain of
cutting her away from the all-inclusive nature of life.
Although the Great Mother embraces everything, She
requires that Her children remain unconscious and
bound to Her in servitude. The spiritual path takes us
beyond the limits of created nature: we become bound
to the Creator and not to His creation. The wayfarer bows
down before no one but God. Detachment is the work
of freeing oneself from the grip of creation while at the
same time honoring its sacred nature.

The alchemists called the process of transformation an *opus contra naturam* because they understood
how the enclosed cycle of nature must be broken for a
higher level of consciousness to evolve. Consciousness
involves separation, and while the feminine honors
the wholeness of life she also needs to break free
from a total dependence upon the Great Mother. The
symbol of *ouroboros*, the serpent eating its tail, images
the realm of the Great Mother in which everything returns
upon itself and the wheel of life keeps us endlessly
imprisoned.

A boy's passage into manhood instinctually frees him from the mother. His spiritual journey is then to rediscover this sacred wholeness within himself. The girl never leaves the arms of the Great Mother, and womanhood is a celebration of her belonging to the creative cycle. A girl's first menstruation symbolizes how she holds the power of creation within her body and can herself become a mother. Learning to become detached can feel like a violation of life's all-embracing nature, and can also carry the guilt that comes with freedom and higher consciousness.

Guilt is a weapon that the Great Mother wields with great effectiveness in order to keep Her children imprisoned. Women, being closer to the Great Mother, are more susceptible to the effects of guilt. For example, a woman who was on retreat became aware that although she loved her husband and children, she was also quite happy alone. This revelation surprised her with a newfound inner freedom, but she quickly felt guilty: "Maybe it is wrong to feel happy being alone when I am a mother and wife." Through such feelings of guilt the Great Mother works to draw Her daughter back into the womb of the collective where she belongs just as mother and wife. The woman at the retreat needed to be reassured of the importance of the new consciousness awakening within her and that it was in no way contradictory to her maternal role.

The spiritual journey is a work of bringing into consciousness our own inner connection to the Beloved. Every soul carries the imprint of His face, the memory of His nearness. Bringing the heart's remembrance into daily life means to consciously acknowledge our spiritual dimension. But consciousness also carries the pain of limitation. The nature of the unconscious is unlimited and undefined. The ocean of the unconscious is without borders or differentiation. The moment something is made conscious it is defined and limited by this definition. To say something is "like this" excludes it from being otherwise. This is against the all-inclusive nature of the feminine. The feminine also knows the danger of definition, how easily life can become crystallized and lose its dynamic, evolutionary nature. The essence of life cannot be fixed or limited, and in the very process of naming what is sacred its eternal nature can be lost. The ancient wisdom of the *Tao Te Ching* expresses this:

> The tao that can be told
> is not the eternal Tao.
> The name that can be named
> is not the eternal name.
>
> The unnamable is the eternally real.
> Naming is the origin
> of all particular things.
>
> Free from desire, you realize the mystery.
> Caught in desire, you see only the manifestations.
>
> Yet mystery and manifestations
> arise from the same source.
> This source is called darkness.
>
> Darkness within darkness.
> The gateway to all understanding.

The feminine knows the mystery and instinctually feels the peril of making this mystery conscious. What the heart knows cannot be understood with the mind. Yet the spiritual path involves the work of bringing together the inner and outer worlds, living outwardly in harmony with one's innermost self. Keeping one's feet upon a path which is "as narrow as the edge of a razor" needs the light of conscious discrimination. We need to see the path as clearly as we are able. Ultimately the wayfarer knows that he cannot know, as in the prayer of Abû Bakr: "Praise to God who hath given His creatures no way of attaining to the knowledge of Him except through their inability to know Him." But in order to live in this world as His servant, constantly attentive to His will, we need to know in the mind as well as in the heart that we belong to Him.

The feminine, attuned to the mystery of what is hidden, can experience consciousness as a cruel and bleak light that brings limitation and misunderstanding. The sacred can seem violated by a harshness that denies both subtlety and change. There is a further difficulty in that the consciousness of our contemporary world is dominated by rationalism and materialism. As a result we lack even the language to describe the qualities of the spiritual. Our language has developed to describe a rational view of a tangible outer reality, and the poverty of language to articulate feelings is an example of our difficulty in describing a fluid, irrational, inner experience. The inner world and its experiences lack the clear divisions which characterize the outer world. Making the spiritual conscious confronts the wayfarer with a collective culture, its language and thought-forms, that have for centuries rejected the sacred in favor of the rational and the material. The limitations of consciousness have never been more evident.

One further difficulty confronting women in our Western culture is the way its masculine and material values in themselves can be experienced as a violation of the feminine. Entering the patriarchal work-place, women are often forced to adopt masculine attitudes and goals that violate their instinctual awareness of the sacred wholeness of life. In order to compete or just survive in today's world a woman may have had to sacrifice her nurturing, maternal self. The emptiness that many people feel in today's material culture can be traced to the fact that the feminine's role of carrying the sacred meaning of life has been rejected and forgotten. The quality of joy that belongs to life lived from a sacred center has been replaced by a search for pleasure. We all suffer from this collective impoverishment, but women, being closer to the core of creation, feel this desolation and violation more strongly. Yet for the same reason more women than men are at the present time attracted to spiritual life. Women feel more acutely the need within themselves and within the collective to remedy this primal pain. But at the same time there is an understandable fear that the mystery which they bring from the soul into consciousness will be again abused and rejected.

A man needs to rediscover what has been lost to masculine consciousness, learn to surrender his instinctual power-drive so that the feminine soul can give birth to the divine mystery. He has to cross the threshold of vulnerability and lay down his sword at the feet of his inner feminine. A woman carries the divine essence in every cell of her body, in the very substance of herself. She needs to bring this sacred self into consciousness despite the fear of violation and pain of misunderstanding. Freeing herself from her attachments in this world, she is able to consciously know and nourish others with the mystery that forms the fabric of her being:

Free from desire, you realize the mystery.
Caught in desire, you see only the manifestations.

CONTRACTION AND EXPANSION

The outer world is a place of both illusion and revelation, a place of attachment and also a place to see the wonder of the Creator, for, in the words of the poet Ghalib, "the world is no more than the Beloved's single face." Yet many wayfarers have to travel through periods when the outer world seems to contract, to become limited, while the inner world opens and gives us a glimpse of the divine. In these periods one often thinks, "Why do I have to live in such a limited way, surrounded by what seems petty and meaningless?" We long to live the freedom we have tasted, but find ourself confronted by outer activities that can feel imprisoning. What we do not realize is that the inner expansion needs to be balanced by an outer contraction. The limitations of everyday life form a valuable framework to help keep our feet on the ground. Otherwise we could easily become unbalanced by the vastness of the inner experience.

When the heart is awakened and we step into the dimension of the Self, we experience a dimension without limitation. The mind cannot grasp the immensity of this reality. We long to disappear into the endless horizon of love. But on the Sufi path we also have to live in the world, be responsible human beings. Everyday life may appear barren and painful, but the heart needs this container. Contraction and expansion work together and form part of the tapestry of the path. The journey takes us further, sometimes deeper into the inner world, or we are thrown back into life.

Then maybe the outer world becomes a place of revelation, as we suddenly glimpse His face, see His beauty in a sunset or the eyes of a child.

So many times I have wanted to remain in one stage of the spiral, to keep the purity of an inner silence uncontaminated by the sounds of outer life; or to remain caught in the soft texture of a dawn, with the sounds of life waking beside a river, waterfowl calling to each other through the mist. These moments of beauty, inner and outer, are so precious, and like cobwebs of dew, so fleeting. One of the most important lessons of the mystic is not to become attached to either inner or outer experiences, not to try and stop the flow of life. From the deep emptiness of meditation one is drawn back into life, into the dramas of being human—yet these dramas can have a deep meaning as well as, often, a seeming madness. While in the fullness of nature's beauty, one is drawn out beyond any form to glimpse His light. Thrown between the opposites, we need to surrender to the flow of experience.

The feminine can reveal to us the hidden face of creation, His name imprinted in His world; and renunciation allows us to turn inward and leave behind the world of forms, to merge within the heart where we can come to know the infinite ocean of love and the dark silence of His emptiness. The mystic embraces everything because "everything is He," and also turns away from all of creation to discover the secret love affair within the heart. The two wings of love take us into a reality that is eternally present and yet hidden. They help us make the journey to the root of the root of our own being where we can glimpse the wonder of our divine nature and come to experience this oneness not just within ourself but within all of life.

Contraction follows expansion just as in-breath follows out-breath. We experience being caught in limitations just as we taste the eternal dimension of our nature. We need the strength of focus and the softness of vulnerability. We need to learn the lessons of detachment and the fullness of life's embrace. The mystic knows that she is in the hands of her Beloved and yet has to stand on her own feet and realize her own strength. The path presents us with these opposites which can seem like contradictions but are contained in the heart's limitless nature.

NO BIRD AND NO WING

Surrendering to the Self, the wayfarer is finally taken into a state of both total inclusion and total renunciation. Everything within the two worlds is held within the circle of the Self, a circle "whose center is everywhere and circumference nowhere." The Self is free from any limitation, any attachment. Free even from the need for renunciation, the lover looks only to the Beloved. This is the state of mystical poverty, the poverty of the heart, whose "inner truth is that the servant is independent of all except God." Mystical poverty is the heart's inner attachment to its Beloved and freedom from outer attachments. It is in this sense that the Sufi regards absolute poverty as absolute richness.

Mystical poverty allows the lover to know his Beloved in the inner and outer worlds. Attached to the world of forms, we see only the outer shape of creation. Unattached to forms, the eye of the heart sees the secret hidden in the outer world, the feminine mystery of creation that came into being with the command "*Kun!*" In the words of 'Attâr,

If the eye of the heart is open
In each atom there will be one hundred secrets.

The Sufi poet Shûshtarî describes how the state of poverty draws the lover into the inner mystery of his own being, where he is able to make the true connection between the outer and inner world and thus realize creation's secret:

> If my clay veils me
>   from my essence,
> the richness of my poverty
>   draws me to me.
> You who seek poverty,
>   if you connect
> the corporeal world
>   with the Secret,
> creation and its mandate,
> the Name will be revealed to you
>   at once.
> You will see the extent
>   of the command—*kun!*—
> and He Who is its Initiator.

Poverty is an inner emptiness which reveals the Name hidden at the core of creation. Within the heart, poverty is a state of annihilation in which there is only the oneness of love. Love's oneness is symbolized by the first letter of the Arabic alphabet, ‌ا (*Alif*), which "represents graphically the straightness, non-deviation and unity of all opposites within the source and beginning of phenomena." This oneness which is both the beginning and the end of creation is eternally present within every atom. For the lover this one letter, *Alif,* is written in fire on the back of the heart. Within the heart

His oneness burns away the veils of duality. Externally the lover may remain in the world of multiplicity, but his love for God has merged into God's love for him. The thirteenth-century Sufi visionary, Najm al-Dîn Kubrâ, explains this state in which the opposites have been united and then dissolved:

> When the lover is annihilated in Love his love becomes one with the Love of the Beloved, and then there is no bird and no wing, and his flight and love to God are by God's Love to him, and not to Him by him.

As we travel the path of love, the opposites spiral inwards towards the center where the two worlds meet. What we know as ourselves, the form of the lover, remains in the outer world of opposites. We feel the fluctuations of the heart, the expansions and contractions of love. But inwardly the states of the lover, the stages of the journey, have been replaced by the effects of the Beloved, "who holds the heart of the faithful between two of His fingers and turns it as He wills." The masculine and feminine aspects of the path are merged into oneness as "the mystic passes away from what belongs to himself and persists through what belongs to God, while conversely he persists through what belongs to God, and so passes away from what belongs to himself."

6. LOVE AND ANNIHILATION

Nothing is possible in love without death.

traditional

TO DIE BEFORE YOU DIE

On the Sufi path the twin threads of love and death are woven together. However, this is not physical death but the death of the ego, as expressed in the *hadîth* "to die before you die." The mystic knows that what separates us from our heart's Beloved is only ourself, as al-Ansârî expresses: "Know that when you learn to lose yourself, you will reach the Beloved. There is no other secret to be learnt and more than this is not known to me." Mystical love takes us beyond ourself, beyond the confines of our ego, until in the ecstasy of union we are lost completely.

Love is the fire that burns us, the passion that destroys us. The soul's love for God frees us from ourself, and yet this freedom can seem like death as we die to the person who we think we are. The lover makes the journey from separation to union, a journey that begins with love and that draws us back to love. This love is given freely and yet there is a price, as al-Ghazzâlî exclaims:

> Not until *two* has been erased
> will lover enjoy union with Beloved.

The lover has only herself to offer, and this is love's sole demand: that we lose ourself, allow ourself to be taken completely and utterly. Mystical love is no idealized romance, but a real passion that requires total commitment, a total giving of oneself to an unknown, invisible Beloved.

This love affair begins with a kiss, a kiss that tastes like wine and intoxicates the soul. Through this kiss our heart is opened and so begins the ancient process of transformation in which the heart is softened. There is a saying that you are a Sufi when your heart is as soft and as warm as wool. Through love we are tenderized, melted, and then merged with our Beloved. One young woman who worked in a hardware store in northern Minnesota came to realize that she was a Sufi after she had the following dream:

> I am in an ecstatic embrace with a lover. There is a tremendous feeling of intimacy and love, and yet it is not sexual. It is the most wonderful feeling of love and tenderness I have ever known. Then I am in a warehouse and at a long table five men sit carding wool. They have long grey beards and they run their fingers through their beards as they card the wool. They are experts at carding wool and have been together for so long that they communicate to each other without talking. One old man twines wool into threads above a figure.

The path which begins with a lover's embrace, with the rapture that belongs to the soul, takes the dreamer into the presence of the old men carding wool. These are the masters of the path, the experts at softening the heart, changing its texture so that it can reveal its secret nature. For centuries Sufi masters have been performing this work, silently, unnoticed. Sufism is a science of love, a deep understanding of the ways of the heart, how to transform a human being through the power and presence of love.

The masters of the path know how to fine-tune the energy of love. And because each heart is unique, on this path no two wayfarers are treated alike. For each of us love comes in its own way, turning us back to our Beloved, infusing us with the energy of union. After I had been with my teacher for about two years I had a dream which she would not interpret. The background to this dream was that about six months earlier the girlfriend whom I had loved since I was fifteen left me. At the time I did not understand why she left me. I remember that when she told me it was time to separate, I just looked into her eyes and saw the love on the level of the soul. I was devastated. I would see her once a week at our meditation meetings, and my heart would cry out across the room. I felt so alone. Then I dreamed I was back together with her and there was so much love. It was a wonderful experience. I waited for her to come back. She never did. After a while she stopped coming to the meetings. About three years later the real meaning of the dream suddenly dawned upon me. In the night, on the level of the soul, I had been with my true Beloved. But I had no image of such love, and so my mind and psyche had interpreted it in a form that I could relate to: I was back together with my girlfriend.

On the Sufi path the real relationship of love happens inwardly, and this can be confusing. Someone once told me about a very disturbing experience in which, while she was half asleep, she had an ecstatic encounter of tremendous passion and love. It wasn't a dream, and she opened her eyes to see who was the man with her in the room. There was nobody there. She was totally unprepared for such an inner experience of love and it terrified her. She had been conditioned to think of love only in relationship to another human being: passionate love can happen only with a human partner.

Mystics know otherwise. They know that an outer relationship is just an echo of the soul's love affair with God. But at the beginning this inner passion can be confusing. We need to develop an understanding of a love that is not between two people. The relationship between lover and Beloved is similar to and yet quite different from a human love affair.

THE SIMPLICITY OF MYSTICAL LOVE

A relationship with God is in many ways simpler and yet more confusing than a human relationship. It is simpler because there are not the drama and psychological dynamics that happen between two people. Human love evokes a complex mesh of projections as deep psychological patterns are activated within each person. We project onto our lover not only our inner partner, but also father- or mother-images, as well as shadow-dynamics and other patterns that all become bonded together. With the Beloved we may try to project father- or mother-images (a distant father, a caring mother), as well as that of lover, but there is not the reality of another person to make the projection stick. We are left with an intangible longing, a deep desire that has no outer object. Loving God has a purity and simplicity that are sadly denied in the complexity of a human relationship. "He loves them and they love Him" belongs to the level of the soul, not to the psyche or the personality.

Loving God, we can give ourself entirely without the danger of being caught in projections or the drama of another's unresolved problems. We are free of the entanglements that belong to two people. And yet there is the primal difficulty of having an invisible, intangible beloved. Where are the arms to hold us, the kiss to intoxicate us? Without any physical presence, how do we know it is real, and not just a fantasy? We live in a culture that only values the tangible, external world. We are bombarded by images that associate a love affair with physical sex. Sufi poetry may use images of physical beauty—"her drowsy eyes," "the curve of her curls," "her ruby lips"—but these are metaphors, and we long to touch with our own hands, to taste with our lips. We long to run our fingers through our lover's hair, to smell a fragrance that is not ethereal.

Yet an inner love affair has a potency that is denied any human lover. We are awakened to this love by a kiss that is *on the inside of our heart.* A kiss on the lips may taste like wine and draw us into our lover's arms, but He kisses us in the most intimate part of our own being, a place so secret that no human lover has access. He kisses us without the limitations of duality, and with a touch that is love itself. From within our own heart He comes to us, opens us, embraces us. Here there are no barriers of protection, but a vulnerability and softness that belong to the inwardness of our own heart. With tenderness and intoxicating sweetness He is present, unexpected and yet longed for, and His kiss is more than one could believe possible. One friend described her first experience of this love: "There are no words for this feeling, which was at the same time a fragrance, a sweetness, and love taken to the extreme of being lost in the Beloved. This fragrance is the most beautiful thing I have ever found in this world—although it isn't a thing, doesn't come from this world, and I haven't found it, it has found me. I want to breathe this sweetness for the rest of my life."

Yet there are days, even months, when the Beloved withdraws and does not show His face, when you are left only with the desolation of your own aloneness. It seems that there is not even a trace of this sweetest fragrance. Then it is easy to doubt this inner love affair and project your longing onto another. With a human lover there is a moment's taste of bliss, a physical knowledge of union. We want what we can hold with our own hands, feel with our body. With the heart's Beloved there is a promise of so much more, and yet it is so intangible, and we are always the victim, always the one who is waiting, as the *Song of Songs* poignantly expresses:

> I opened to my beloved; but my beloved had withdrawn himself, and was gone: my soul failed when he spake; I sought him but could not find him; I called him but he gave me no answer.

In this love affair all of our patterns of seduction, the games we play to keep our lover, are useless. We become so vulnerable. We are love's prey.

In human relationships we have been taught to look after ourself, to draw boundaries and not to be victimized. We know that we shouldn't be taken advantage of, that we shouldn't be violated. This is very important, learning to keep our human integrity and sense of self, not to sell ourself for what appears as love or the promise of security. But the ways of mystical love are very different. In the relationship with our soul's Beloved we have to give ourself without restrictions, and we are violated, abused, and loved beyond compare. We are taken by force, abducted and transformed, and we give ourself willingly to this self-destruction through love. The poet John Donne expresses the paradoxical nature of divine love in the phrase "nor ever chaste except thou ravish me." We are purified through love's violation; we taste our own union through love's destruction.

A friend had a powerful and simple dream evoking the difference between a human and divine lover. Although she is offered "the man of her dreams," she is drawn further into a deeper, more dangerous relationship:

> I am on my way to heaven. I know I am going there. I am in a large hallway, walking. I come to an opening, a large beautiful area with beautiful people. A wonderfully gorgeous man calls to me. I think this must be heaven, but then I know it is not because I am physically drawn further down the passageway. I want to stay, but I must go on. The man comes to me. He is gentle, kind, and so beautiful to look at. I cannot stop, for if I do it would be like hell.
>
> I continue to the other end of the hall. It opens up into nothing. It is like a great void. I am very frightened, scared to death. Did I make a mistake? I don't want to go in—there is nothing there. I am drawn in. I must go in. There is suddenly an incredible pressure on my chest. It hurts. I can't breathe. I know that it is the foot of God. I wake gasping for breath.

Seeking the ultimate lover, she is drawn into the void, into the nothingness of mystical love. She is scared, terrified of the depth of her heart's call and what awaits her. Mystical love is not a gentle courtship, but a passionate affair that demands all of our self, in which every pattern of self-preservation is torn down. She awakes gasping for breath.

Love takes us by force beyond every limit, beyond what we think is possible; we are tortured and made whole by love—time and time again we lose and rediscover ourself, only to fall deeper and deeper into love's endless abyss. Rûmî, who through Shams came to know the intoxicating intensity of this real love, describes how it is given freely and yet takes us into a vastness that can seem like death:

> subtle degrees
> of domination and servitude
> are what you know as love
>
> but love is different
> it arrives complete
> just there
> like the moon in the window
>
> desire only that
> of which you have no hope
> seek only that
> of which you have no clue
>
> love is the sea of not-being
> and there intellect drowns
>
> this is not the Oxus river
> or some little creek

this is the shoreless sea;
here swimming ends
always in drowning

a million galaxies
are a little scum
on that shoreless sea.

Love's ocean is real and endless, a place not for the fainthearted, not for those who like security or safety. The mystic is seduced and dragged into this love, seduced by its softness, dragged by its power. This love abuses our sense of self, destroys our patterns of control, violates our deepest beliefs, and takes us back to God. In this love there is neither form nor limit, only a completeness beyond even our dreaming, a sweetness beyond imagining, and a terror that belongs to the absolute. Love takes us into the infinite emptiness of His presence, into the vastness that is hidden within our own heart.

The mystic is someone who gambles on this love, who gives her life to love's longing. There is no safety net for disappointed lovers, no self-help group for those caught in this fire. The path of love is described by Saint Gregory of Nyssa as "a bridge of hair across a chasm of fire," and what happens when you come to the middle of this bridge? The fire burns the bridge and you fall into the depths, into the flames. This is why the Sufis call the lane of love a one-way street. Once this primal passion has been awakened the lover cannot return to the rational world, to the world of the ego. You can only give yourself, and give yourself, and give yourself.

The sensible man never goes near to this fire, but remains within the safety of the known. There is a Persian song whose words are:

> Don't come near to the Lane of Love!
> It is not a thoroughfare!
> You cannot sleep, you cannot eat; you don't
> enjoy the world anymore!
> Don't even look in the direction of the Lane
> of Love!
> What can I do? Helpless I am.

This love is an addiction as potent as poison. It destroys everything we once held precious; everything that seemed important is burnt in its flames; we hunger for just another taste of this love which is destructive and so sweet—nothing else matters. The values of the world fall away as this inner love affair takes hold of us, a passion a thousand times more powerful than any human love. In a human love affair there is always the safety of our own self: we are separate from our lover and can withdraw. But our soul's Beloved does not belong to duality, as Rûmî writes: "He is closer to you than yourself to yourself." Can we hide from our own heart, can we run away from our own life's blood? We can try, we can attempt a thousand patterns of distraction, but if we just turn inward He is waiting for us, offering us the sweetest torture, the softest death.

Love's death is real, and yet we remain alive, sometimes limping through the days. We are addicted to an inner lover who demands everything and yet so often leaves us devastated and alone. He awakes in us a hunger for what is real, and then seemingly abandons us. The inner deserts through which lovers travel are desolate beyond belief, just as the moments of intoxication are bliss upon bliss. Once you give yourself to this poison there is no going back, because the world has lost its attraction. You are like Majnun, the madman, the lover, who cried,

> Oh who can cure my sickness? An outcast I have become. Family and home, where are they? No path leads back to them and none to my beloved. Broken are my name, my reputation, like glass smashed on a rock; broken is the drum which once spread the good news and my ears now only hear the drumbeat of separation.
>
> Huntress, beautiful one, whose victim I am—limping, a willing target for your arrows. I follow obediently my beloved, who owns my soul. If she says "Get drunk," that is what I shall do. If she orders me to be mad, that is what I shall be.

These words may seem like poetic exaggeration, but anyone who has given herself to love knows their truth. Each in our own way we are taken by love. Sometimes an external relationship can open our heart—maybe a hopeless love affair pierces through our defenses. But once we are gripped by the heart's true passion then the real sorrow of the soul comes to the surface, the soul's longing for its only Beloved. This longing is the dark side of love that drags us to the abyss, and it is also the sweetest poison because it reminds us of our true Home. We become, like Majnun, an outcast, a traveler on love's dusty highway.

GAMBLING ON LOVE

The path of love does not follow the ways of the world;
nor is the lover even interested in salvation, as Râbi'a
said: "Oh Lord, whatever share of this world Thou dost
bestow on me, bestow it on Thine enemies, and whatever share of the next world Thou dost give me, give it
to Thy friends—Thou art enough for me." We are not
prepared to wait until we physically die to be with our
Beloved. We are willing to give away our whole self to
be with Him now. And the mystic knows it is possible,
knows in her heart the truth of living in the presence
of God, of an intimacy that is known only to His lovers—the wonder of His softness within the heart, of
being suddenly filled with ecstasy, of simply knowing
that you are loved without restriction.

At the beginning such love may seem like a dream,
a distant possibility. Our heart is touched and we don't
know why; a longing is awakened that seems to have no
source. This is when we must gamble and give ourself
to this longing. Many times I have met people who had
such longing and yet were frightened to give themself;
they held back from this great adventure. Their rational
sensible self provided them with many reasons; life offered other paths to travel. This is the moment for risk-
takers, for crazy fools who are bored with security and
need to be reckless. Rûmî knew this dangerous love:

> A lover doesn't figure the odds.
>
> He figures he came clean from God
> as a gift without a reason,
> so he gives without cause
> or calculation or limit.
> A conventionally religious person

behaves a certain way
to achieve salvation.

A lover gambles everything, the self,
the circle around the zero! he or she
cuts and throws it all away.

This is beyond
any religion.

Lovers do not require from God any proof,
or any text, nor do they knock on a door
to make sure this is the right street.

They run,
and they run.

A SIP OF WINE

Divine love is a very corruptive power because it destroys all of the ego's patterns of control. Our ego spends
so much time and energy validating itself, protecting
itself, defending itself against anything that might
threaten its position, justifying its own importance.
Love takes us down a different road, and as the poet
E. E. Cummings wrote, "love is a deeper season than
reason." While the ego continually tells us what is right
or wrong, helpful or disturbing, love slips through
the cracks in our defenses, bewilders and confuses
us. Love offers us another way to live, beyond our expectations and outside of our control. The following
dream tells of how the inner lover comes like a wind,
invading the dreamer's home, leaving her frightened
and powerless:

> I feel a sense of danger, some man who wants
> to come into my house. I close all the windows
> and shutters of my house. But when I go to the
> back door it is open and a wind is blowing into
> the house. I know that a dangerous man is in-
> side, but I don't see him. An artist in the house
> is able to make a sketch for the sheriff. He
> sketches a ghost-like figure in which all that
> can be seen are two piercing eyes that seem to
> go on forever.

We may try to call the sheriff, to keep love away, to keep safe in our house, but love has other plans. Without knowing why, we leave the back door open, the place in the unconscious where love can always enter. Love comes "like a thief in the night" and steals us from ourself, from our safe, secure life, dragging us into the unknown. Love is the wind of the spirit which "bloweth where it listeth," a force beyond our control.

Love can be violent or soft. Sometimes she seduces us, tempting us with soft kisses and the fragrance of a hidden secret, like a scented breeze from a summer garden. Al-Hallâj, who was love's martyr, said that God takes us "either by a lure that seduces or by the violence that forces... and God shows better through that which seduces, for a lure is superior to violence." In the West we have forgotten the mystery of divine seduction, how love comes and takes us by the hand and leads us to the fire. But the Sufis have always known about this aspect of the path, how we are trapped by the musky tresses of our Beloved, or how her bewitching eyes cast a spell we cannot break.

We are conditioned to have control of our life, but then love takes over, and we have to surrender, to allow ourself to be tempted. The righteous person may fight against temptation, but Sufis are not interested in being righteous; they are interested in melting in love "like sugar in water." Love frees us of ourself, merging us back with our Beloved:

Love came
    flowed like blood
        beneath the skin, through veins
emptied me of my self
    filled me
        with the Beloved
till every limb
    every organ was seized
    and occupied
till only
    my name remains.
    the rest is It.

Love draws us to love, pulls us into this sweet abyss, melts away our attachments, drowns us in ecstasy. Who would not give away everything for another taste of this intoxicating substance? The Sufis say that one sip of this wine and you are lost, you would sell everything for just another sip. They speak of the "tavern of ruin" where love's wine is given freely; the only price is yourself, your sanity. But the lover gives herself gladly, such is the potency of love's temptation, such is the unbelievable sweetness of this embrace. The first time I felt the butterfly wings of love at the edge of my heart, I knew I was given more than I thought could ever be given. And later the love came again, richer, deeper, more complete, more intoxicating. All one can think is, why me? What have I done to deserve this? And the heart is so grateful.

I remember the look on a friend's face as he told me how he had awakened that morning to find love in his heart, a love that had just arrived, that didn't come from anyone else. In his heart there was just love. And I knew that his life was changed forever, because now he knew, he knew that love was complete, and free, and forever. This friend had prayed and meditated for years, but he never expected something so simple, so pure, so wondrous. My teacher describes how it first happened to her:

> And so it came.... It tiptoed itself into my heart, silently, imperceptibly, and I looked at it with wonder. It was a still, small, light-blue flame, trembling softly. It had the infinite sweetness of a first love, like an offering of fragrant flowers with gentle hands, the heart full of stillness and wonder and peace.

The miracle of love awakening within us takes us by surprise, and in this love we are lost and found and lost again. There is no before or after, only the sweetness of a moment. So many nights we have cried our longing, so many tears have been shed, but all of our suffering is so little compared to what we are given. Our own Beloved has come back to us, has not betrayed us, has emptied our heart and filled it with sweetness.

PURIFIED BY LOVE

On the path of love there are many stages, times of desolation and moments of nearness. Once love has seduced us, once we have surrendered ourself to her seduction, we are taken along this ancient road that is within our own soul. Love draws us back to love. There is a beautiful *hadîth* which describes how love takes us through the stages of the journey:

> Verily, Almighty God has a wine for His friends, such that when they drink of it, they become intoxicated, and once they are intoxicated they become merry, and once they are merry, they become purged, and once they are purged they become melted down, and once they are melted down, they become purified, and once they become purified they arrive, and once they arrive they become united with the Divine, and once they are united with the Divine there is no distinction between them and their Beloved.

The wine of love seeps into the human being from the innermost chamber of the heart, what the Sufis call "the heart of hearts." This is the hidden place that belongs only to the Beloved, to which no one else can have access. Here the soul knows that she belongs to God and lives in the love of His presence. Once we taste just a sip of this wine we remember how we are together with God; we are awakened to love's deepest secret. This one sip immerses us for an instant in union, intoxicating us with a love that we will never find in the outer world of duality. The danger of this sip is that it awakens a thirst for what the world can never give, a love known only to God's idiots, those who are prepared to sacrifice the world and even themselves for just another sip. Nothing in this world is as addictive as divine love, a love that empties us of everything except our Beloved. When one friend was about to join this caravan of lovers, she dreamt that she was injecting herself with heroin.

She awoke from the dream horrified until she realized its deeper meaning.

The wine of His love is only given to those who are prepared to be addicted, to have their whole structure of consciousness broken down, to become His own personal idiots, the fools of God. This wine fills us with a crazy happiness, the happiness of the soul that is going Home, that is no longer going to remain caught in the prison of separation. This wine challenges all the values of the world and purifies us; love tears down the veils of illusion, the barriers of our own defenses, until we stand naked and vulnerable. We are purified by longing, by the tears that our heart cries, and so we are melted down. The pain of love makes us inwardly abandon everything we hold precious, our attachments, even our beliefs. We become so thirsty for just another sip that we sell or give away everything—nothing else matters. Even our self-respect, our self-worth—all is destroyed, dissolved, melted by love and longing.

The purification of love is both painful and ecstatic. We often think of purification as belonging only to ascetic practices, fasting or abstinence. But love's purification is more potent, more joyous, and more devastating. Love confronts us with our repressed pain and darkness and then clears away the debris of our life. Then she throws us into an abyss both blissful and terrible because it has no limits, no boundaries. In this abyss everything is left behind, even ourself. Love teaches us that we do not matter, that only our Beloved has substance. If in moments of human passion we can forget everything, how much more powerful is divine passion, the love affair with the king of Love?

We have come to think of love just as an emotion, a feeling, and forgotten that it is the most powerful force in creation. Once we give ourself to love, once we say "yes" to this crazy passion of the soul, love takes us in its grip. Rûmî tells a story of a village teacher,

> who was so destitute that during the winter he had nothing but a length of linen. By chance a flood had caught up a bear in the mountains and swept it down with its head under water. Some children saw the bear's back and cried out: "Teacher, here is a fur coat fallen in the ditch. Since you are cold, take it out." The teacher was in such need and so cold that he jumped into the ditch to get the fur coat. The bear dug its claw into him and held him in the water. The children cried, "Teacher, either bring the fur coat out, or if you can't, let it go and come out!"
> "I've let the fur go," he said, "but it won't let me go! What am I to do?"

THE JOURNEY IN GOD

Love is alive and grabs the poor lover, taking us downstream, far from our own village. In this process we are purified and arrive back where we belong. Love takes us Home into the arms of our Beloved. Through love we make the journey from forgetfulness to remembrance, from separation to union, from ourself to our Beloved. Then the journey of annihilation, *fanâ*, becomes the journey of *baqâ*, the journey in God. Everything up to now has been a process of preparation for being with our Beloved. Fakhruddîn 'Irâqî describes this journey:

> Beloved, I sought you
> here and there,
> asked for news of you

> from all I met;
> then saw you through myself
> and found we were identical.
> Now I blush to think I ever
> searched for signs of you.

Once we have tasted the real mystery, that the Beloved is in our own heart, then we wonder how we could have looked for Him elsewhere. Why did we even need to look for what is always within us, is a part of the very fabric of our soul, the essence of our own essence? We searched and searched, and in this searching, love took us by the hand and dragged us away from our ego back to our real nature; again to quote Fakhruddîn 'Irâqî:

> If you lose yourself
> on this path
> you will know in certainty
> He is you, you are He.

How can we be separate from Him who is everything, when every atom of our body bears His name, when every flower and leaf sings His praise? The ego tricked us into thinking that He is separate from us, but now the ego has been burnt, drowned, lost. Love has taken over: "my self tied up its bundle and left." The veils of illusion are lifted and love reveals her hidden face, the oneness of lover and Beloved.

The Sufis may use the term annihilation, but the ego remains—one cannot live in this world without an ego. Without an ego I would not know that I am separate from my neighbor, I would not even know that I exist. But the ego ceases to take center stage in one's life. More and more it moves to the sidelines, busying itself with daily affairs but no longer being the main actor. Instead, in the center of oneself there is a space for something else, something that cannot be defined but belongs to love and to the infinite emptiness from which love comes into the world. The following dream describes a lover in service to his Beloved, waiting at the edge of the world:

> I am at the edge of the world. On my left side is the world, all full of light. On my right side all is dark and black. Out of the darkness pure love comes into the world. At this moment I know that this is His game and I have nothing else to do but play it by His rules as He wants. It is His game and I have to play it as He wants.
>
> I experience a great longing to go into the darkness, but I realize that I have to wait until He takes me inside the darkness. Until then my job is to wait at the edge of the world and give everything I see to Him.

Sometimes we experience the sweet companionship with our Beloved: sometimes we just live the ordinariness of everyday life. But always we are in service. Once we know love's truth we no longer belong to ourself. We are here for His sake. The journey in God may take us deeper into the dark silence of love, the nothingness that lies behind creation, but in this world we belong only to Him and are His servant.

Love's union is stamped within the heart, and our own self is the only veil that separates us from this mystical secret. Once love has brought us Home, we realize the illusory nature of our ego; we come to know how we have always belonged to love and love's king. The ego, battered into surrender, melted down by longing, steps aside and allows us to glimpse this truth. We are taken into the place of merging, where we dissolve into love. Deeper and deeper we are lost in love, and there is no end to this journey, because love has no end. This love has no form, just the infinite emptiness that is beyond the mind and the senses, and yet this emptiness loves us, loves with a tenderness and passion that are known only to His lovers.

The journey back to God is love's journey in which our desire for God unites with His desire for us. The mystic gives herself to this deep, primal desire of the soul, a desire that destroys what we think we are, that takes us into the whirlpool of our own heart where we are drowned and discovered, are lost and found. Why is it such a painful journey? Because, in the words of a Persian song,

> The ego will not go with laughter and with caresses,
> But must be chased with sorrow and drowned in
> tears.

But love is more powerful than all of our evasions, than all of the walls we have erected around us. And because our desire for Him is part of His desire for us, once we say "yes" love perfects itself within our heart and soul; in the words of Mechthild of Magdeburg:

> And God said to the soul:
> I desired you before the world began.
> I desire you now
> As you desire me.
> And where the desires of two come together
> There love is perfected.

7. PRIMORDIAL NATURE

Each creature God made
Must live in its own true nature;
How could I resist my nature,
That lives for oneness with God?

Mechthild of Magdeburg

THE SONG OF CREATION

Just as a sunflower follows the sun, so does each particle of creation inwardly turn towards the Creator. Everything that is created praises God. This is the song of the universe, the harmony that underlies everything. Without this song there would be no life, no existence: the world would fall apart. Prayer and praise are our natural state of being, the heartbeat of our soul. And yet, for most of us, this is something we have forgotten and have to work to rediscover. We have to rediscover the music of our own soul, the primordial song of our own being.

Every cell of creation knows God, as Henry Vaughn beautifully expressed: "Every bush and oak doth know I AM." This inner orientation towards God is instinctual. His name is stamped in every cell of our body, which knows that it came into the world to praise Him. In praising Him we acknowledge that He is Lord; He is the one we love and adore. We are a part of Him and we come into this world in order to praise Him, to sing His song of love.

What is the purpose of creation? Why did He who is one and alone, perfect and pure, create the world? Although we can never presume to know the ways of God, the Sufis say, "I was a Hidden Treasure. I longed to be known so I created the world." From the unknowable oneness were born the myriad wonders of the creation. What is visible reflects what is invisible. The creation in all its beauty and violence reflects the primordial oneness of the Creator. The purpose of creation is to reveal the Hidden Treasure that we call God. This purpose is held like a seed or embryo within every particle of creation. His longing to be known is the deepest force of nature.

The song of creation is a song of praise. We hear it in the songbirds at dawn, see it in the first flowers opening in the spring. It is in our response to the beauty of a sunset or the glimpse of snow-capped mountains. At moments like these the heart opens in recognition of something we cannot name. For a moment the veils between the worlds lift and the beauty of this world awakens a memory of the inner beauty our heart knows but we have forgotten. We sense the song of praise that is in the spinning of every atom and in the motion of the stars. This praise is the imprint of His name in His creation. It is life's memory of its source. Dhû'l-Nûn describes his experience of the creation's own song of praise:

> Whoever recollects God in reality, forgets all else beside Him, because all the creatures recollect Him, as is witnessed by those who experience a revelation. I experienced this state from evening prayer until one third of the night was over, and I heard the voices of the creatures in the praise of God, with elevated voices so that I feared for my mind. I

heard the fishes who said, "Praised be the
King, the Most Holy, the Lord."

To praise Him is to witness that He is the Creator. The
act of praise is the creation's recognition of its Creator.
It was because He longed to be known that He created
the world. In praising Him the creation tells the Creator
that it knows Him. To praise Him is the esoteric, or hidden, purpose of creation, the most primal genetic print
without which the universe would dissolve.

The act of praise is an act of remembrance that is
the dynamic center of creation, and yet mankind has
forgotten this. We do not understand nature's deepest
secret—"There is nothing that does not glorify Him in
praise, *but you do not understand their glorification*"
(Qur'an 17:44). We have forgotten that everything remembers Him. We have forgotten that the act of praise
does not have to be learnt but is an instinctual part of
our very nature. The cells of our body praise Him, the
neurons in our brain know Him, and yet this is held
secret from us. We have to relearn what all of creation
constantly sings.

In becoming conscious, humanity lost touch with
its instinctual knowledge of Him. Consciousness (eating of the fruit of the tree of the knowledge of good
and evil) banished us from paradise, from a state of
unconscious oneness with all life. Nature sings the song
of oneness without the burden of consciousness. A
stone, a flower, or an animal is itself and is in harmony
with the whole, a wholeness that is not limited to the
created world but also embraces the Creator. Nature
unknowingly reflects its Creator, the Hidden Treasure,
for "the world is no more than the Beloved's single
face."

We speak of the ecological oneness of nature, but there is a deeper oneness that nature embodies. The oneness of nature is a reflection of His oneness. Nature instinctively knows this inner, unmanifest wholeness just as a child instinctively knows its mother. But in nature this knowledge is not conscious. Consciousness is born with the pain of separation, with the banishment from paradise. With a child the birth of consciousness heralds the experience of separation from the mother, and the longing to return to paradise is often identified with the mother-complex, the longing to return to the nurturing oneness of the mother. As consciousness grows so does the sense of our individuality, and the maturing of individual consciousness in adolescence is accompanied by the need to reject the parental world, in particular the world of the mother. Consciousness creates a drive to express individuality that is bound together with the need to separate. Without separation there can be no individuality, but the shadow side of this drive is the experience of isolation. The pain of consciousness is the pain of aloneness, and the more conscious we become, the greater our sense of aloneness.

Consciousness carries the pain of separation from our own instinctual self, and with it the separation from our instinctual knowledge of the Creator. God walked in the Garden of Eden, but when Adam and Eve had eaten of the fruit of consciousness they hid themselves from Him and were then banished into the wilderness. This wilderness is life without the sense of oneness. When we feel cut off from nature or from our own instinctual self, it is this exile from a sense of oneness that haunts us.

In our contemporary society the sense of alienation from what is natural has reached an extreme. We place great value on self-expression and individuality but what appears more dominant is a collective feeling of isolation, futility, and meaninglessness. Both our inner cities and our inner selves carry the stamp of a collective desolation. Like an abandoned child we long for our mother, for life's nurture and sense of wholeness. Drugs have captivated us with their promise of paradise, the brief moment of ecstasy and forgetfulness. What our material culture cannot give us we seek in this shadow-land of self-abuse. The pain of consciousness has the quality of a purposeless agony which we seek to escape through pleasure or addictions.

THE PURPOSE OF CONSCIOUSNESS

The primal purpose of consciousness is to praise and to know Him. To this design great temples and churches were built, rituals and music performed, sacred books written and studied. Until the advent of rationalism in the seventeenth century, the pursuit of knowledge had a spiritual foundation. Its underlying objective was to come to know the Creator and His creation more fully. In the last three centuries we have forgotten this heritage, and our materialistic culture and its companion greed have increasingly dominated the world. Consciousness has been enslaved by the desires of the ego and we have lost touch with its deeper spiritual purpose.

None knows God but God. But in His creation aspects of Him are made known, what the Sufis call His names and attributes. When we look towards God, when we praise Him, we give this knowledge back to Him. The created world does this naturally. Sometimes one can glimpse this in meditation, or in the silence of nature—how every atom sings His song, sings His name. But mankind has the ability to do this consciously, knowingly. We have the ability to make conscious our natural state of being, our innermost harmony with God.

There was a state, before the creation, when we were together with God. The Sufis call this moment the "Primordial Covenant" when God asked the not-yet-created humanity, "Am I not your Lord?" and humanity replied, "Yes, we witness it." Our soul's covenant is to witness that He is Lord. This is the primal purpose of consciousness, to know Him and to praise Him. For this purpose He gave us His greatest gift, the gift of consciousness. Consciousness is what separates us from the natural world. And with consciousness comes free will. As much as we have the ability to remember Him and to praise Him, we have the ability to forget Him. We have the ability to use consciousness only for the purposes of the ego, for our own personal pleasure or benefit. As a culture we have become so engrossed in the pursuit of ego-consciousness and the wonders of our material culture that we have forgotten our deeper purpose. We have forgotten that we are here to praise Him.

Praising God, we do not deny our individuality, but we offer it back to Him whom we love. We use our consciousness in its highest capacity: to reflect what is highest. And in our praise and prayer we come to know our own divinity. At the Primordial Covenant we pledged to remember Him, to acknowledge that "He is Lord." This pledge is stamped into our soul, and when we consciously remember Him and praise Him we feel the depth of our belonging to Him; we come to know the soul's secret—that we are a part of God and reflect His oneness. Our own individual nature at its deepest level is an embodiment of His uniqueness. In our prayer and praise, in our meditation and practice of remembrance, we live our true individuality for His sake. We offer ourself back to our Beloved and come to realize how we are made in the image of God.

Life takes us from the maternal oneness on a journey of discovery as we come to know our own individual self. We are driven by a longing to know who we are as a unique individual and to express this uniqueness. But the journey continues as we feel the deeper need to go Home, to offer our individual self back to God. We are awakened to the pain of separation and feel the anguish of the soul that is separate from the source, the lover separate from her Beloved. On this journey back to divine union we do not return to the unconscious oneness of the mother; rather we come to realize the true nature of our individuality. As a unique expression of His uniqueness we can live this quality, not for the purpose of ego-gratification, but as an expression of Him whom we love.

Life offers us the experiences we need to come to know our own individual self, and our spiritual practices are a way to offer this self back to God. Our outer life and inner practices work together. In our daily life each time we remember Him we are making a conscious offering of ourself. Our remembrance is a connection through which we look towards Him and give of ourself. We use our consciousness for its highest purpose. Alone in meditation we can give ourself completely back to God. In the Sufi meditation of the heart we surrender our whole self to our heart. Drowning the mind and its thoughts in the love within the heart, we sacrifice our conscious self on the altar of love. In the moments of deep meditation we are lost completely. There is no individual consciousness: we have given it back to God.

Giving ourself to God, losing our mind in the ocean of His love, we discover our essence, our innermost state of union with God. Paradoxically we only realize the essence of ourself when we give ourself away. While the ego has to hold onto its notion of individuality, protect itself from others, the nature of the Self is realized through surrender and sacrifice. The Self is the part of our being that is not separate from God, and yet also carries our true individuality, our unique note in the symphony of life. Through giving ourself back to oneness, the oneness of God that is also the oneness of life, we are taken to our essence; we experience His unique stamp within our heart. While the mind thinks "I can only realize my individuality if I am separate," the heart knows the deeper truth that the soul's individuality is only realized through a state of union.

THE SECRET FACE OF CREATION

Within the heart, love draws us back to oneness. The heart knows and lives this oneness. Through the heart we have access to oneness, and love takes us from separation to union, from the knowledge of our own self to being lost in God. Love comes from the beyond and carries the stamp of oneness: that He and His creation are one. This is why love is like a magnet that draws us from duality back to oneness. We experience this in human love, how we want to get nearer and nearer to the one we love: emotionally we want to merge, physically we want to unite. Love is a force that pulls us towards union. In human love we are always limited by the fact that there are two people. In divine love there is no such limitation. In meditation we can give ourself completely, merge into the ocean of love, experience the complete oneness that is found within the heart.

In meditation we give ourself away, lose our self in the ocean of His oneness. In this state there is a death through which we can live the secret of the soul, the oneness of lover and Beloved. And in this oneness we find what is really ours. Not the illusion of our ego-self, but the reality of our true self, the self that knows that it is one with God. Returning from meditation, we bring this innate knowledge into consciousness. The work of the path is then to live this oneness, to live the knowledge of the heart in everyday life. Then the song of the soul becomes a part of the texture of our life, the prayer of the heart is lived in each moment. In our outer activities as well as in our inner attention we witness that He is one, we praise our Lord.

Living this deepest prayer and praise, we offer our unique self back to our Beloved. We live our true individuality—not the illusion of separateness that belongs to the ego, but the stamp of His uniqueness that belongs to the soul. We live our real self as a note in the great symphony of creation, the song of the oneness of everything. The Great Artist created the world as an expression of His uniqueness. All of creation knows and honors this; and each leaf, each raindrop, each created thing glorifies Him just through being itself, as Gerard Manley Hopkins beautifully expresses:

> As kingfishers catch fire, dragonflies draw flame;
> As tumbled over rim in roundy wells
> Stones ring; like each tucked string tells, each
>   hung bell's
> Bow sung finds tongue to fling out broad its name;
> Each mortal thing does one thing and the same:
> Deals out being indoors each one dwells;

Selves—goes itself; *myself* it speaks and spells,
Crying *What I do is me for that I came.*

The deepest purpose of individuality is to offer
its uniqueness back to its Creator. Through prayer and
praise we live our uniqueness in the presence of our
Lord and so bring into consciousness this primal connection of the soul, the instinctual harmony that is at the
foundation of all of life. What other purpose can we have
than to praise Him? How else can we come to know the
fragrance of His love for us, the mystery hidden in the
garden of creation?

As a culture we have forgotten this secret face of
creation, this natural orientation of our own being. Instinctively we look towards God, instinctively we know
that He is Lord. But each of us in our journey has to
rediscover this, has to uncover what all of creation lives.
We have to return to the root of the root of our own
being to discover our own natural state of prayer, our
own natural way of being with God. We each praise
God according to our own unique nature. The musi-
cian may praise Him in his music, the athlete in her
body, the shopkeeper in the way he helps his custom-
ers, the mystic in each moment of remembrance. But
in the silence of the soul the same great symphony is
being played: the complete oneness of all of creation.

The journey of self-discovery takes us first to our
own individual self, and then deeper into the circle of
oneness. Through meditation and prayer and everyday
life we come to realize the tremendous mystery of how
our individuality is an expression of this oneness, how
everything is a meaningful part of the whole. One stormy
evening in New York I was giving a talk to a handful of
people, and someone in the audience asked the important question about how to integrate one's inner search

with one's contribution to outer life. A black woman in the audience who had been encouraging me throughout my talk by frequently exclaiming, "Hallelujah, O Lord," and "O Yeah," whenever she agreed with something I said, took it upon herself to answer this question. With deep instinctual wisdom she explained, "You have in your heart a map that was put there when you were in paradise. When you go into your heart you will find this map, and as you open it you will find that it fits together with the maps of those around you, all forming part of a larger map."

Within the heart there is a wholeness that embraces all of life. In the heart is found the soul's blueprint that carries the purpose of our incarnation, the note that we can play in the great symphony of creation. As the heart looks towards God, we are able to live from this map that carries the imprint of our Beloved. Returning to the heart, we join the unity of life that acknowledges He is Lord. Here is our natural state of being which we can access through prayer, meditation, and devotion. Within the heart we are able to be with ourself and with our Beloved. The heart contains the circle of creation in which everything looks towards the center where the Creator reflects Himself into His world. The philosopher Plotinus describes how only when we look towards the center do we participate in "that free and conscious co-operation in the great life of All which alone can make personal life worth living":

> We are like a choir who stand round the conductor, but we do not always sing in tune, because our attention is diverted by looking at external things. So we always move around the One—if we did not we would dissolve and cease to exist—but we do not always look

towards the One. Hence, instead of that free and conscious co-operation in the great life of All which alone can make personal life worth living, we move like slaves or marionettes, and oblivious to the whole to which our little steps contribute, fail to observe the measure whereto the worlds keep time.

THE WILL TO WORSHIP

It is said that a human being incarnates with two primal desires: the will to survive and the will to worship. All other desires are added afterwards, a product of our parents, environment, and other conditioning. The will to survive is our instinctual orientation to life, to the horizontal dimension of our existence. Survival drives us to find food and shelter, to satisfy our physical and emotional needs. The will to worship is the vertical dimension of our existence, the way the soul instinctively looks towards God. In many previous cultures the will to survive and the will to worship formed an integrated tapestry of work and ritual that was the basis of life.

In our Western culture the dominance of science has emphasised the horizontal dimension to such a degree that we have become unbalanced. We may be surrounded by the physical benefits of science that have taken our ability to survive to new levels of comfort and complexity. But we have sadly lost touch with our natural need to worship, with our instinctual orientation towards prayer. We live in a culture in which the secular and sacred are kept separate. As a society we no longer honor the sacred, and many people feel this inner poverty without knowing its cause.

The spiritual journey takes us inward where we rediscover the simplicity of being with God. As our heart opens we experience our need to look to our Beloved, to live in communion with our Creator. What has been lost in our outer culture we find within ourself; we rediscover our will to worship. But what is most precious is that when we find this natural orientation of our being it no longer carries the limitations of any imposed form. Instead of any collective religious structure, we discover our own unique way of being with God. Our journey has taken us beyond the collective into the dimension of our true individuality to where our heart sings in praise, to where we can hear the unique music of our own soul.

The journey that drew us into discovering our individual self takes us back to where we can experience the deepest purpose of this self. Our uniqueness is realized as a part of the whole, as a woman glimpsed in the following dream:

> In that place of not being awake and not being asleep, I heard a chorus of women's voices and I had the impression of women in the sky who were coming in a v-formation, and they were singing the most heavenly music—it was incredible, beautiful. And then one of these women did a virtuoso; it was as if her voice soared out from the rest of the chorus. And if you've ever heard a bird give its all to a song with incredible trills and swelling of the chest that's what this woman did. I remember lying there and hearing her voice and the range was incredible. She would swoop down and reach its lowest note and then soar up...

As the dreamer awoke she realized that the singer was herself, and the song was her own self in praise. This is the same glorification as Mary's, "My soul doth magnify the Lord," when she gave thanks that His child was conceived within her. He calls us to Him and then gives birth to Himself within our heart, and what is born is our own primordial state of prayer and praise.

But there is a price to be paid for this awakening: the comfort of the collective. The journey towards true individuality is a journey away from the collective. Our Western culture may appear to support individual expression. Yet this expression is allowed only within the prescribed norms of the collective, as anyone who seeks to follow "the path less trodden" discovers. For example, on the inner journey dreams are an invaluable guidance. But how easy is it to be guided by one's dreams in an environment that only accepts what is tangible and rational? Our everyday world seems to have little place for the symbolic wisdom of our dreams. The clamorous demands of our "normal" life drown out the subtle music from within. As we awaken into a regulated world of time and space the mysteries of the soul are pushed aside. Our dreams then remain just a forgotten interlude in a demanding, competitive world, whose material values have no place for the hidden path that has unfolded for us in the night.

Dreams reveal our own unique journey which we have to fight to rediscover. Like St. George battling the dragon, we have to struggle to free our virgin self from the grip of the collective. The collective is threatened by real individuality. The moment you step away from the collective, not as a rebel who is in fact just acting out the shadow of the collective, but as a seeker of individuation, you challenge its power. The collective often responds by making you feel guilty, for example with arguments that the inner journey is just a selfish pursuit. Guilt and patterns of dependency are two of the most potent weapons of the collective, and it is a master of deceit and deception. The collective can bombard you with doubts as you struggle to discover what is your real nature. Who has not felt the power of thoughts that emphasize security, the importance of career or possessions, heard the voice that says you are crazy to follow your dreams, that you are just being deluded and fanciful?

To be an individual is to break the primal taboo of the collective, and every wayfarer knows the pain and sense of isolation this creates. This sense of isolation is emphasized by our Western culture because it has long denied the mystic. Since its early struggles against the gnostics, the Christian church has rejected the individual quest in favor of social and political power. Where is the wandering dervish or orange-robed *sannyasin* of our culture? The seeker's tendency towards isolation is even more emphasized in the United States, which, being the most extrovert society in the world, has little sympathy for the introvert path of the mystic.

Only too often the outcast carries the shadow of the culture, which for the mystic is the unrecognized longing for something beyond the material world. Those who belong to the Beloved carry His curse which is the memory of His embrace. Nothing in the world will fulfill them. But when this curse is combined with the collective shadow it can easily become a feeling of shame. How many children are silently worried because they see a world invisible to their parents? How many adolescents bury their spirituality because it has no echo? These feelings fester in the darkness. They become the secret shame of the shadow. We sense the emptiness of material values. We see that the emperor has no clothes. But without an outer context to contain or help us understand this insight we are left only with the primal guilt of consciousness. Spirituality thus carries a double curse.

Shame is a particular affliction for women. Shame has long been a tool of collective patriarchal repression. In our Judeo-Christian culture woman was blamed for banishing us from the Garden of Eden, and since then women have been made to feel ashamed of their instinctual self, of their bodies, of their femininity, and also of their spiritual nature. Feminine spirituality carries the sacred wholeness of life, which has been despised and rejected by the masculine which longs to escape the limitations of the physical world. For many women a deep, imposed shame comes to the surface and has to be faced.

Not everyone has the strength and determination to painfully struggle through the barriers of the collective. To sing the song of our soul demands a sacrifice of many accepted values, and also requires that you become free from one of the most potent forces of our culture, the drive towards ego-gratification. The journey to the source takes us away from the surface and the many artificial stimulae that dominate contemporary life. But if we are able to break free of the grip of the collective we discover something so natural and pure within us. We return to the place where we know and are known by God, as a three-year-old girl poignantly reminded her mother when she told her how she spoke to God at night. She just said, "God, I know." And God replied, "Yes, and I know."

THE CALL TO PRAYER

Within the heart the soul looks towards God. The journey Home calls us here, to where we are always in a state of prayer and praise. We hear this prayer within our heart and it attracts us. It calls us away from confusion back to simplicity. Love's call draws us inward to where the music of the soul can be heard. Our work is to listen, to become attuned to love and to hear this secret song of the soul amidst the distractions of the outer world and the chatter of our thoughts. Learning to listen is to open ourself to what is most natural, to the heart's call to prayer. Returning within ourself, we find that prayer is a natural state of being that has been hidden from us. We feel the grace and joy of looking towards God, of being part of the great whole of creation that praises the Lord. We take our true place in the circle of life and love.

Once we hear the *muezzin* within the heart calling us to prayer, singing the eternal song of "He loves them and they love Him," we need to follow this call. We need to catch the thread of our own devotion, of our own individual "mode of prayer and glorification." The prayer of the heart needs not just to be lived in the inner recesses of our heart, but to infuse itself into our daily life, so that what has been hidden is brought into consciousness.

Every atom of creation praises God, every cell is infused with divine remembrance. This is the bond of love that holds the world together; it is the hidden axis of creation. But while all of creation instinctively knows that He is Lord, only mankind has the capacity to make this knowledge conscious. He gave us the gift of consciousness so that we could remember Him, so that we could bring the hidden knowledge of the heart into the light of day. In the depths of the heart we know Him, but through our acts of devotion we can make this knowledge conscious and so fulfill our deepest purpose.

The path takes us back to the core of our being, back to where His name is engraved into our very being. We respond to the call of love, the call of our Beloved who longs to be known. Making this journey, we turn away from the collective to walk the solitary path of the pilgrim, the path that leads each lover into her own heart. Within the heart we come to know our own way of being with God, our own way of witnessing His oneness. We bring this knowing back into our daily life where we make an offering of our unique self. We consciously commit ourself to the work of remembrance, to the practice of prayer, to acknowledge that He is Lord.

A life of praise and prayer is demanding and free-ing. It demands our utmost attention and our commit-ment to the secrets of our own heart. It frees us from anything that separates us from our Beloved, for, to again quote al-Hallâj, "when Truth has taken hold of a heart She empties it of all but Herself." Within the heart we discover our true uniqueness. This is not the unique-ness of the ego with its illusory demands for freedom and self-expression, but the unique way our Beloved has textured our heart, the unique way we can reflect His uniqueness.

Such is the freedom of the Sufi path that it allows us to live our own way of being with God. The fewer the outer forms of the path the greater the freedom. He who is formless finds His way into our hearts and into our lives. The path guides us inward, takes us from the confines of the ego to the greater wholeness of the Self. Then the power of the path gives us the strength and protection we need to live a life of prayer and devotion in the marketplace of the world. The lover has to stay true to her Beloved amidst all the distractions of everyday life. In the words of Abû Sa'îd ibn Abî'l-Khayr,

> The perfect mystic is not an ecstatic devotee lost in contemplation of Oneness, nor a saintly recluse shunning all commerce with mankind, but "the true saint" goes in and out amongst the people and eats and sleeps with them and buys and sells in the market and marries and takes part in social intercourse, and never forgets God for a single moment.

The heart of the lover always remembers her Beloved. Without this remembrance, days are empty and meaningless. Those who are drawn to the path of love are called to the work of remembrance. Their duty is to praise and remember Him. They bring the note of divine remembrance into the symphony of creation and help to keep the world attuned to love. His lovers stand at the core of creation and sing the song of lover and Beloved.

Because our culture only values what is tangible and rational, we have forgotten the greatest mystery of being human. We have forgotten the secret hidden within our own heart. As a civilization we have lost touch with our natural way of being with God. The mystic is drawn to rediscover this secret, to free himself from outer attachments and conditioning so that the way of the heart can be lived without restriction. The simple intensity of this purpose is stamped into the consciousness of the soul, and it pulls us into the fire of love, the fire that purifies and transforms us. Love's fire awakens the heart, drawing us back to what we had forgotten, our natural state of belonging to God.

We are a part of creation and once the heart is awakened we live the primal destiny of knowing to whom we belong. The creation looks towards its Creator and the heart looks towards God. We feel the oneness that unites all of life, and feel how we are a part of this oneness. We know that there is nothing other than God, that His oneness is stamped in every leaf and rock. We have been awakened to His presence and we look towards Him in love and praise. We belong to Him since before the beginning of time, and now, in His world, we come to know it.

8. LIGHT UPON LIGHT

Light rises towards light and light comes down upon light,
"and it is light upon light."

Najm al-Dîn Kubrâ

THE HEART BELONGS TO GOD

Sufism is a science of love, of the mystery that is hidden within the heart. In the center of the heart, what the Sufis call the heart of hearts, is the light of divine love. This light belongs to God and is placed within the heart for the purpose of lighting the way Home. The wayfarer is one who walks this path, who is guided by the light hidden within the heart.

In our world we have forgotten that the heart belongs to God and that the mystery of love is His mystery. The mystic is one who reclaims this mystery, who acknowledges that the heart belongs to the king of Love. To quote the tenth-century Sufi, al-Hakîm at-Tirmidhî:

> God placed the heart within the cavity of the human chest, and it belongs to God alone. No one can have any claim to it. God holds the heart between two of His fingers, and no one is allowed access to it: neither an angel nor a prophet; no created being in the whole creation. God alone turns it as He wishes. Within

> the heart God placed the knowledge of Him
> and He lit it with the Divine Light.... By this light
> He gave the heart eyes to see.

The path of love takes us into the heart of hearts, into the arena of His love where He holds the heart of His lover between two of His fingers, as expressed in the *hadîth*, "The heart of the faithful is held between the two fingers of the All-compassionate. He turns it as He wills." Sometimes He turns our heart towards Him and we feel the tenderness of His intimacy, the bliss of His nearness. Our heart melts with the warmth of His loving. And sometimes He turns our heart away from Him and we experience the desert of separation, the cold emptiness of desolation. Living with your heart held between two of His fingers is an intensity of surrender in which you are entirely dependent upon your Beloved. You have given yourself into His hands, not just your outer life, but the depths of your heart, the core of your being.

When the heart is held between two of His fingers we experience an inner state of surrender and prayer. Mystical prayer has a quality of belonging and total dependency which the lover lives in each moment. Our heart belongs to our Beloved and He does with us as He wills. We have given ourself to God so that He can use our heart for His purpose: as a sacred space where He can reveal Himself to Himself, where the secret of *light upon light* can take place.

With love and devotion we polish the mirror of our heart; through inner work we cleanse our heart of impurities. The purer our heart the more we are able to surrender, to give ourself to our Beloved, because it is the impurities of our ego-self that hold us back, veil us from God. The grip of the ego is what keeps us from entering into the sacred space of the heart of hearts where we know that we belong to God and are instinctually surrendered. The more we work upon ourself the closer we come to experiencing this secret of the heart, this natural state of surrender. Finally His light begins to break through the clouds of our ego-perception, to disperse the doubts and difficulties that surround us and absorb so much of our attention. Then we are able to glimpse the wonder of belonging to God and give ourself more and more completely to this belonging, to this miracle of mystical loving.

In His light we see the light of our devotion, the depths of our longing. As our heart becomes clearer and clearer so our Beloved uses it as a mirror, a mirror in which He can see His own face and reflect His light into the world. This is the essence of mystical service, of living in surrender and prayer. "There are servants among My servants who love Me, and I love them, and they long for Me, and I long for them and they look at Me, and I look at them ... and I see what they bear for My sake and I hear what they complain from My love."

THE ILLEGAL ACTIVITIES OF LOVE

His light falls into our heart, and the light of our loving, of our longing and our devotion, looks to our Beloved. This is the esoteric mystery of *light upon light*: "Light rises towards light and light comes down upon light, '*and it is light upon light*.'" There is an enigmatic passage in the Qur'an (24:35) which the Sufis have interpreted as a metaphor for this mystery of the heart:

> God is the Light of the heavens and the earth,
> His light may be compared to a niche

wherein is a lamp
the lamp in a glass
the glass as it were a glittering star
kindled from a Blessed tree
an olive that is neither of the East nor of
    the West
whose oil would almost shine forth
though no fire touches it.
Light upon light
God guides to His light whom He will.
God speaks in metaphors to me.
God has knowledge of all things.

Within the niche of the heart shines the light of His love. The mystical journey brings us to this place of devotion and prayer, because it is His will. He guides us back to our own heart.

One friend had a dream in which he goes on a journey into the jungle, up a river back to its source. There is a risk involved in making this journey, and the dreamer has left behind a good life, and good friends, and family. On this journey he meets the natives who are in harmony with the natural, spiritual rhythm of the place. At the same time there are Western colonial "authorities" who try to suppress the activity of the natives. They have just killed two natives, who were engaged in "illegal activities," by cutting out their hearts. But despite the danger and difficulties, the dreamer goes with the natives and comes to a place where a light shines down from a mountain top. And then he sees that a corresponding light comes from a rock beside him, "as if a laser beam passes between the two points." Around him are the natives, their attention fixed on the light that comes down from the mountains. They seem to be quietly chanting, and their sound fills the landscape. The dream ends with a sense of awe and spirituality.

The dreamer had recently retired from a successful corporate life, and the dream describes a journey to rediscover his natural spirituality, though it would involve risks and leaving behind the outer values of "a good life, and good friends, and family." In his journey through the jungle the dreamer begins to become attuned to the dance of the natives, and it is with their natural, spiritual movement that he makes his way upriver. This dance is the natural rhythm of the soul, in which we learn to live in harmony with our deepest being. This is the dance of primitive rituals and also the joyous clapping of an infant's hands. It is the joyous dance of creation, the eternal "yes" that sings in the blood, without which there would be no blossoms on the trees or light in a lover's eyes.

This dance is a state of prayer, a natural way of being in which we praise Him, but it has been outlawed by a masculine culture striving to dominate nature. When the Puritans banned the maypole dances because of their hedonistic, erotic qualities, our culture repressed the earth's sacred dance in which fertility and praise belong together. We are born in order to praise Him, and in this act we are not separate from the rest of His creation. Within everything that is manifest, His song of love can be heard.

The dance of the natives in this dream is the soul's celebration of its divinity, the devotee's response to the heart's call to prayer. But the "authorities" are active in "suppressing" this "activity" and two natives have had their hearts cut out. The heart is our spiritual center, the home of the Self, described in the *Upanishads* as the abode of "that Person in the heart, no bigger than a thumb, maker of past and future." Without a heart there can be no connection with our eternal nature, no feeling of the infinite. By "cutting out the heart," the authorities of the collective have denied us access to our innermost being; they have locked the door of love that opens into His presence.

This action poignantly symbolizes our material culture's desire to imprison us in the temporal world. The mind and the ego can be conditioned, as the advertising media exploit to its fullest impact, but the heart cannot be collectively controlled. While the mind often expresses thoughts programmed by outside influences, the heart is its own master and often surprises us with unexpected feelings.

The heart contains the organ of our spiritual consciousness and the Self is its guardian. In the innermost chamber of the heart there is a place that no human being can reach, not even one whom we love. The mind and the ego cannot disturb this space or influence it with any desire. It belongs only to Him. Here, in our heart of hearts, we are in a constant state of prayer. If the door to the heart is closed, we lose contact with this state of communion.

In our extrovert culture the spiritual ways of the heart have been forgotten. Love's intimacy has become a term for sexual passion, and the idea of a divine lover is found only in myth or the fantasies of romance novels. A friend dreamed that she was living in her parents' house and her lover came and rang at the door, bearing a bouquet of flowers. She opened the door and invited him in, but there was nowhere that they could be alone together. Her inner lover had come to her with the gifts of love, with symbols of her spiritual flowering. But in order to be alone with her heart's desire and experience the tenderness of His touch, she needs to leave the house of her conditioning, where there is no room for such intimacy. The heart's longing needs a space of seclusion, a place for spiritual communion to unfold.

We each need to find an inner space where we are not disturbed by social values that tell us that we should be doing something practical and that the heart's vulnerability will lead only to pain. Opening to love, we open to the pain of love as much as to its bliss, but that is the price of being His lover. We give ourself to a love that does not belong to the world, to a longing that will take us to our real home.

GIVING BIRTH TO LOVE

The dreamer has made the journey upstream to the source, to the root of the root of his own self. Here he witnesses the mystery of *light upon light*, as a light shines down from the mountain and a corresponding light rises from a rock beside him, while the natives attentively look towards the mountain.

The light on the rock beside the dreamer is the light of his own inner Self which connects with His light high in the mountains. Through the fire of our longing the light within the heart rises to meet His light and His light comes to meet us. This is the secret of the mystical communion, the journey of the soul back to the source, as the thirteenth-century Sufi, Najm al-Dîn Kubrâ, describes:

> There are lights which ascend and lights which descend. The ascending lights are the lights of the heart; the descending lights are those of the Throne. The lower-self [the ego] is the veil between the Throne and the heart. When this

> veil is rent and a door opens in the heart, like
> springs towards like. Light rises towards light
> and light comes down upon light, *"and it is
> light upon light"* (Qur'an 24:35)....
>
> Each time the heart sighs for the Throne,
> the Throne sighs for the heart, so they come to
> meet.... Each time a light rises up from you, a
> light comes down towards you, and each time
> a flame rises from you a corresponding flame
> comes down towards you....

We each come into the world with a spark in the heart, but it soon gets covered by the dust of the world. Then, when the moment is right, the Beloved looks into our heart and reignites the spark of divine love, and the mystery of *light upon light* commences. The light in the heart rises to God, creating the feeling of longing, and this longing in turn attracts His light. The greater the longing burns within the lover the more it attracts the attention of the Beloved: "Each time the heart sighs for the Throne, the Throne sighs for the heart, so that they come to meet...." This is the secret of the heart's sorrow, and why longing is the golden thread that takes us home. Within the heart of His servant He calls to Himself, and He answers His own call: "I respond to the call of the caller when he calls to me" (Qur'an 2:186).

The flame of longing that burns within the lover is His light in the world. The flame polishes the mirror of the heart until He can see His own face in the heart of His servant. This polishing is the inner work and the pain of the path which wear away the lover until only the Beloved remains.

The heart is the womb of our spirituality. The heart of the lover belongs to his Beloved, and it is within the heart that the mystery of union is conceived and born.

The light from above and the light from below meet, and in this meeting He lifts the veils of separation and reveals the secret of divine love; the lover experiences being united with God. Through the tears of our longing He gives birth to Himself within the heart of His lover, as Rûmî expresses: "Sorrow for His sake is a treasure in my heart. My heart is *light upon light*, a beautiful Mary with Jesus in the womb."

Our work is to be attentive to the needs of love. Often people have dreams in which they give birth to babies but then neglect them. The child of the heart needs to be nourished with prayer, meditation, and re-membrance. This is the mother's milk for our divine child. Through these practices and our aspiration the heart opens and we are able to receive the light from above, the "manna" that comes direct from the source.

The work of the lover is to stay true to the longing and remain focused on the source. In a dream a friend asked her Beloved what she could do for Him, and He simply replied, "Be there for Me." If we remain inwardly attentive to the needs of the heart, we attune our whole being to His purpose, to love's unfolding. This attention is a natural state of prayer because we are doing what our own heart desires. It is not imposed upon us by any outside influence. Rather it is consciousness following the call of the heart rather than the desires of the ego.

Najm al-Dîn Kubrâ explains that the "lower-self," the ego, is the veil between the Throne and the heart. This veil is "rent" when we seek a deeper fulfillment than the ego can offer, and stay true to this seeking. Surrendering ourself to the path, to our longing, we go beyond the ego. When we meditate we surrender the mind to the heart, to the power of love. Then the mystery of *light upon light* begins, a process so different from the ego's drive for self-gratification that this inner dynamic cannot be understood by the rational mind. The heart knows but the mind is increasingly left in a state of confusion. We leave behind the logic of the world of duality and enter into a reality that can only be explained by the language of merging and union.

The light within the heart of the wayfarer is nourished by His light and grows until it is the same as the light from above, for "as above so below." The light above and the light below merge in a state of oneness in which the soul is paradoxically both united and unique, both absorbed and its own individual self, as al-Hallâj expresses in these famous lines:

> I am He whom I love, and He whom I love is I.
> We are two spirits dwelling in one body.
> If thou seest me, thou seest Him;
> And if thou seest Him, thou seest us both.

MERGING IN LOVE

The mystery of *light upon light* is something so different from the reality of the mind and the ego and their patterns of attachment and desire. The mind often remains in confusion, unable to understand the wonder that is taking place within us. One just has to allow oneself to be bewildered. Something is happening within which we cannot grasp, which does not belong to the limited understanding we have of ourself. A process is taking place beyond the realm of the mind. These are the illegal activities of love which rational consciousness tries to suppress.

The language of the heart is so different from the language of the mind, because the mind understands through separation, through one thing's being different

from another. But the heart understands through nearness, through intimacy, and finally through union. So
lovers speak in images and metaphors. Mystics speak
of absorption, of "melting in meaningfulness like sugar
in water," of drowning in an ocean of love. And yet
in this melting, in this drowning, we are both lost and
found. When everything has been lost, when all trace
of our own identity has been dissolved, the real secret
of being a human being is revealed.

Once we have been merged with our Beloved, the
journey back to God becomes the journey in God. We
are united with the Beloved and yet we remain ourself.
Spiritual life becomes a state of oneness and duality.
Within the heart we have tasted union, we have given
birth to His oneness. And yet in our outer life we remain in duality and offer ourself to God in service and
surrender. "My soul doth magnify the Lord" describes a
state of duality. In praise and prayer, in longing and
love, our light rises to our Beloved. And His light comes
to meet us, and it is *light upon light*. The mystic lives
the mystery of *light upon light*, and in this meeting
there is oneness, a oneness known within the heart but
bewildering to the mind.

In waking consciousness we live in His world of
duality which in the heart we know to be one. We surrender to separation, as expressed in the Sufi saying,
"I want union and He wants separation. Therefore I
surrender to separation so that His wish comes true."
Only through being separate can we praise Him and
serve Him. Through the mystery of separation we can
come to know the wonder of our Beloved, His power
and beauty, and so fulfill the deepest purpose of His
creation.

The mystic lives the paradox of love, the tension of
union and separation. In our longing and prayer His

hidden treasure is revealed: in the words of Ibn Arabî, "We give Him birth by knowing Him in our hearts." We participate in the miracle of His divine birth within us. Within our heart the spark of the heart rises to meet the fire of His love and the meeting of *light upon light* takes place. Giving ourself to the heart's desire for God, we partake of this inner happening, the union of the soul with God.

A STATE OF BEING

The journey Home takes us to where love is perfected, to the center of ourself where we are eternally connected to God. Entering this sacred space brings a sense of awe. Like Moses before the burning bush, we take off the shoes of our outer life as we sense the greater mystery of the soul. Here is the essential fire of our being that is always pure and undefiled. The energy of this inner core of light and love is at too high a frequency for it to become polluted by the thought-forms of the world, by psychological problems or ego desires. This is the sacred chamber in which the fire of His love for us is always burning.

The path takes us into this inner arena, and here we are absorbed in love. Here we die to ourself, to the ego, in order to partake of the deeper wonder of being human. For many years of preparation the lover waited on the outside of this chamber. When we are ready, when we have polished the mirror of the heart, the door opens and we are drawn by love into love. We can resist. We may fight the heart's desire with complaints and doubts and patterns of self-protection. We can identify with our ego-self that is to be abandoned, lost, burnt. And the ego will cry out and resist with all of its skill and strength of protest, crying "What about me?" But the pull of the heart, the attraction of *light upon light*, is stronger because it carries the power of the Self. And our work is to surrender, to go, like al-Hallâj, gladly to the gallows of love.

The spiritual path is a vortex of love that pulls us beyond ourself, that draws us into an abyss in which our ego-self is abandoned, what the Sufis call the "tavern of ruin." The more the wayfarer identifies with the path, gives herself to the currents of love, the less power she gives to the ego and so the faster it falls away. When does the ego go? When the lesser is absorbed by the greater, when the Beloved takes us into His arms and we are lost in love.

To be lost in love is a wonderful state, without worry or desire. We discover how we are always with God. This is our natural state of being. Sufism is not taught with words. It is a state of being that is reflected from heart to heart. Within the heart we know that we are with God, and our ego, our sense of separation, is left behind. We need the ego to function in the world, to live in this world of duality. But within the heart we have been immersed in the deeper knowledge of our real self. He has revealed Himself to us within our own heart.

Spiritual life is a state of being, a natural state of being with oneself and with God. Because it is a state of being we can never find it, but through our searching we tear away the veils that separate us from this consciousness of the heart. What we discover is that we know how to be with God. A familiarity and awe, an intimacy and distance are woven into the substance of the soul. Each of us will experience and express this state of being in our own way, for, as it is said in the

Qur'an, "Every being has his own appropriate mode of prayer and glorification."

Within us we discover the way the Beloved wishes us to be with Him, and then we allow that state of being into our life. In our individual way we mirror His uniqueness. Rûmî tells the story of Moses who overhears a shepherd praying,

> God,
> where are You? I want to help You, to fix Your shoes
> and comb Your hair. I want to wash Your clothes
> and pick the lice off. I want to bring You milk,
> to kiss Your little hands and feet when it's time
> for You to go to bed. I want to sweep Your room
> and keep it neat. God, my sheep and goats
> are Yours. All I can say, remembering You,
> is *ayyyy* and *ahhhhhhhh*.

Moses, affronted by the shepherd's natural intimacy with God and way of addressing Him with such everyday language, criticizes the poor shepherd, who tears his clothes, sighs, and wanders into the desert. But then God comes to Moses, and says:

> *You have separated Me*
> *from one of My own. Did you come as a Prophet*
> *to unite,*
> *or to sever?*
> *I have given each being a separate and unique*
> *way*
> *of seeing and knowing and saying that knowledge.*
>
> *What seems wrong to you is right for him.*
> *What is poison to one is honey to someone else.*

Each in our own way we learn to love Him, to give ourself in love to Him. The gestures of lovers are intimate and individual. As God says to Moses, what matters is not the form of expression, but what is within, the attitude of the lover, the fire in the heart: *"Forget phraseology, I want burning, burning."*

After God has spoken, Moses runs after the shepherd and, finally catching up with him, says,

> I was wrong. God has revealed to me
> that there are no rules for worship.
>   Say whatever
> and however your loving tells you to....

But the shepherd in his loving has gone beyond any form and he thanks Moses,

> You applied the whip and my horse shied and jumped
> out of itself. The Divine Nature and my human nature
> came together....

The return journey takes us through the world of forms into the formlessness of His presence. Through our acts of devotion, our longing and perseverance, our own individual nature is melted and then He merges into us. This is one of the greatest mysteries. The Beloved merges into the lover, the ocean flows into the dewdrop.

When the door of the heart is opened, His infinite emptiness enters. What remains of His servant becomes a shell. Everything else is burnt away, dissolved in the currents of His love. The more our attention is with God, the more we are made empty for His sake. The deepest prayer is without words. The most primal praise is silence, a silence in which the very being of the lover is increasingly absorbed somewhere, far beyond the mind and the senses. The Beloved needs us to make known to Himself His own non-being, His essential emptiness. We are made empty because He is empty. In our emptiness we bring this hidden treasure into the world.

9. THE TIMELESS MOMENT

The Sufi is the child of the moment.

traditional

This moment in which the soul is smitten
This is a moment in which life, for me, is worth the universe.

'Attâr

DIRECT REVELATION

One of the most important archetypal figures in Sufism
is Khidr, "the green one." Khidr represents direct revelation, the direct inner connection with God that is
central to the mystical experience. The mystic is someone who needs to have a direct inner experience of
the divine; in the words of one Sufi, "Why listen to
second-hand reports when you can hear the Beloved
speak Himself?"

While the conventionally religious person may as-
pire to follow the religious law, lead a virtuous life, and
seek salvation, the mystic is driven by a need for direct
spiritual experience, by a primal desire for union with
God. Khidr is the inner figure who gives us access to
this inner reality; he is the archetypal mediator who
is the remover of obstacles and opens the door to our
heart's desire.

Khidr appears in the Qur'an in a story in which he
is not referred to by name, but as "one of Our servants

unto whom We have given mercy and bestowed knowledge of Ourself." Khidr is one who has direct knowledge of God, and his traditional color of green reflects this because in Sufi symbolism green is the color of the realization of God. Khidr has drunk of the waters of immortality and he appears to the wayfarer at times of greatest spiritual need. However, Khidr traditionally appears as just an ordinary man, and only after he has departed does the wayfarer realize his true nature.

The Qur'anic story of Khidr begins with Moses searching for Khidr, because, according to a traditional version, the people have asked Moses if there is anyone who knows more than he does. Moses, who often represents the outer, exoteric, religious way, replied that he didn't think that there was, but then God tells him that there is someone and he can be found at the place where the two seas meet. Another sign that Khidr can be found here is that at this place "the cooked fish becomes alive again." Moses wants to learn from Khidr and together with his servant goes in search of him. Along the way he passes by this place. Only later, when they stop for their morning meal, hungry from their journey, and discover that the cooked fish has swum off into the water, does Moses realize that they have passed the place they were seeking, and so they retrace their footsteps.

Moses seeks direct spiritual knowledge, the inner mystical connection with the divine. But from the beginning his journey is not as it appears. He passes by the place "where the two seas meet," where the inner and outer worlds come together, and only when he is hungry does he realize his mistake. The mystical connection is where the two worlds meet, the spiritual and the temporal. The mystical journey takes us to this place within ourself, to this umbilical cord connecting us with the divine, but one of the very first lessons is that it is not as it appears. How often, even with the best intentions, do we blindly pass by this place, do we miss the thread of our inner connection? Only when we stop because we are hungry do we realize our mistake.

We all have our own preconceptions about spiritual life, about how the path will be for us. For some it means to be in a loving and caring environment, for others to have a sense of direction, to find clarity in their life. Each in our own way we are drawn onto the path, we go searching for Khidr. Maybe along the way, caught in our preconceptions, we will pass the place where the two seas meet, the mystical rock where the inner meets the outer and divine grace comes into our world. Rûmî says, "Don't look for water, be thirsty," because it is our innermost need, the hunger of the soul, that reminds us of what we have lost, that draws us like a magnet to the place of our unfolding, to where the heart can open.

Khidr is the spiritual teacher within us, the spark in the heart, our inborn secret. And one of the mysteries of the path is that Khidr is always present, is always our invisible companion, and yet we need to find the right environment to meet him, to become open to our own innermost self. We meet him at the place where the cooked fish becomes alive, where the spiritual tradition becomes a living reality. When I first met my teacher and looked into her eyes I knew that *she knew*. I knew with certainty that this old woman with piercing blue eyes lived on the further shores of love. In her small North-London room with the passing trains rattling the windows, divine love was alive. Here was a presence that spoke directly of the mysteries I had heard hinted at in the books I had read, a fragrance of an inner reality beyond the mind and the senses. For me this was the place where the two seas meet, where the cooked fish became alive, where my heart started to spin.

I was so hungry, starving for a nourishment that the world could not give. I had read books and practiced yoga and meditation. I had even had a few mystical experiences, but I did not have access to the direct connection of love that could take me Home. I did not even consciously know what I needed. I had been brought up in a middle-class Christianity that has no concept of a living mystical tradition. But my soul knew what it wanted and drew me to the path that would nourish me, to this secret place where the two worlds come together, and I no longer felt like a stranger, an outcast in a world I did not understand.

For each of us, for everyone drawn onto the path of love-longing, there is this place where the spirit can open us to the divine, where we can come into contact with Khidr. How do we recognize it? The heart knows even if the mind does not. I knew that I had come home, had found something for which unknowingly I had been looking. My desperation had drawn me to an old woman and a spiritual group where divine love flowed into the world, where grace was tangibly present. My need had been answered and I wearily laid down my heavy bundle and was grateful. My mind did not interfere, did not even question what had happened. I was fortunate in that I had no doubts. I just felt a sense of belonging I had never believed possible. Since then I have met others who are bombarded by doubts: "Is this the right path? Is this my teacher?" The difficulty is that the mind can never answer such questions, but will only pose more questions, create more difficulties. To catch the thin thread of our mystical journey is rarely easy, and we do not always recognize what we have been given.

WHERE THE TWO SEAS MEET

We find Khidr at the place where the two seas meet, where the cooked fish becomes alive. Here, where the two worlds intersect, is a place of grace where the timeless moment is present. In this moment the eternal dimension of the soul becomes accessible and the real mystery of the inner journey begins. The timeless moment is real and dynamically alive, and belongs to neither past nor future. This is the vertical dimension of our own self, in contrast to the horizontal dimension of the ordinary world of the senses and the mind.

In the temporal world we are governed by the past and think of the future. Our past often imprisons us with patterns and habits, and seems to determine our future. The timeless moment belongs to the heart, to the eternal now of love, to the freedom and fear of a life without restrictions. In the moment we belong to God and He is present, while in the past and future we belong to ourselves and our conditioning. Only in the moment can we have access to our real self, because our essence does not exist on the level of the mind and its illusion of time. The mystical journey begins when we open the door to the timeless moment and leave behind the security of what we know. Whether we make this journey depends upon whether we can follow the way of Khidr or will remain caught in the learnt attitudes of the mind and the ego.

In the story told in the Qur'an, Moses asks Khidr:

> "May I follow you so that you may guide me by that which you have been taught?"
> "You will not be able to bear with me," Khidr replied, "for how can you bear with that which is beyond your knowledge?"

Moses said, "If Allâh wills, you will find me patient; I shall not disobey you in anything."

Khidr said, "If you want to follow me, you must not ask any questions about anything, until I myself speak to you about it."

And the two set out.

The first statement of Khidr, "how can you bear with that which is beyond your knowledge?", confronts the wayfarer with a central quality of the mystical journey— it is beyond what we know. The mystical path is not about knowledge but about a state of being, about living from the essence of oneself. On this journey we know neither where we are going nor how to get there. When I first met my teacher I had read many spiritual books and thought I knew something about spiritual life. But suddenly I found myself confronted by a reality which my mind could not grasp, which had to do with an old woman who lived in the presence of God and radiated a love which was not of this world.

I gave away my small library of spiritual books and for ten years read only novels and poetry. In my teacher's small room amidst the circle of friends I felt something I could not name, could not understand, and fortunately my mind did not try. For years I just went to the meetings, meditated, drank the offered cups of tea, and listened to her talk. Yet I remember very little of what was said, just sensed the presence of her teacher, her Sufi sheikh, and the power of a living mystical tradition. What was given was beyond my understanding.

The mystical path is the *via negativa*, the way of not knowing. Once we come to the place where the two seas meet, we have to leave behind all our conceptions, and gradually we forget what we thought was important. Mystical life is totally different from anything we could imagine or expect. It does not belong to the past or future, but to the still center of ourself. The heart is awakened and draws us away from our ego-identity into a quality of being that is so simple because God is a simple essence. Through the heart, through the presence of the path, we lose what we thought we were and discover something eternally wonderful. In the words of 'Attâr,

> What you most want,
> What you travel around wishing to find,
> Lose yourself as lovers lose themselves,
> and you'll *be* that.

We become what we are and slowly we learn to live this quality of being. We learn the ways of Khidr.

THE NEED OF THE MOMENT

But what about all the questions, all the doubts and difficulties with which the mind bombards us, with which we subtly undermine our aspirations? As the story of Moses and Khidr continues, Moses cannot help but question Khidr who acts in a way that appears incomprehensible. First Khidr bores a hole in a ship, then he kills a young man, and finally he repairs a wall in a town of inhospitable people. Each time Khidr rebukes Moses for his questions: "Did I not tell you that you wouldn't bear with me?" After the third incident Khidr says that they must separate, since Moses cannot abide by his promise, and then tells Moses the reasons for his actions: how the ship belonged to a poor fisherman and would have been captured by a king who was seizing every boat by force;

how the young man was a criminal who would have committed many crimes; how the wall belonged to two orphan boys, and underneath the wall was a treasure which God had decreed they should discover when they grew to manhood.

Finally Khidr explains to Moses, "What I did was not by my own will." Khidr is surrendered to God and acts on His behalf. He does not question the will of Allâh. He acts as he is directed, according to the need of the moment. The rational self cannot accompany such an inner attitude and Khidr parts from Moses. If we are to stay with the path we must leave behind the mind and its doubts: we must part company with our rational self. The mind remains but our allegiance is to a higher power, and even our doubts cannot dissuade us. Our doubts may attack us, they may cunningly try to convince us of the need for rational explanation, but the heart knows a deeper secret.

When our doubts try to distract us it is better not to enter into an argument, because the mind loves confrontation, and has an endless succession of questions. Instead the wayfarer learns to accept the limitations of the mind and gradually becomes free from the grip of its arguments. We come to recognize its repetitions as familiar and boring. The patterns of the mind do not belong to the moment, to the quality of being that is our true nature.

Often when a person first comes to a Sufi group he has many questions. These initial questions may be valuable and help the wayfarer understand the new sense of direction, the way the path appears to work. It is best not to repress these questions, as then they just fester in the unconscious. In a Sufi group some questions are answered directly, sometimes the answer is hinted at, sometimes the wayfarer is left to find his own way to the answer. Unasked questions may also be answered. But slowly as the energy of the path infuses itself into the wayfarer's consciousness, the questions fall away. We lose the need for explanation as we become immersed in love's silence. Many times people have told me how they came to my teacher's door with questions on their mind, only to have these questions dissolve or fall away in her presence.

Moses' quest for knowledge took him to the place he sought, where the two seas meet, but then he encountered a different reality in the figure of Khidr. Now questions are to be left behind if Moses is to learn from his guide. The attitude now required of Moses is one of surrender, acceptance, and patience. He has to bear with that which is beyond his knowledge. He has to follow without judgment or understanding. For every wayfarer there comes this moment when we have to leave behind our patterns and preconceptions in order to be open to the will of God, in order to catch the thread of a deeper unfolding. Moses forgot his promise to be patient and not to question his guide, and so was not able to follow Khidr. How many times do we forget this promise that we make to ourselves, and like Moses judge situations by their outer appearance? In the eternal now there is no past upon which to make our judgments, only a response to the need of the moment, the hint from God imprinted into the heart. The way of the Sufi is to live from this center, to be a "child of the moment."

A NATURAL WAY OF BEING

The way of Khidr is both an inner mystery and a practical reality. Learning to live without judgment, without being caught in outer appearances, allows the wayfarer to respond to the need of the moment. In the words of al-Makkî, "The Sufi acts according to whatever is most fitting to the moment." Free from the patterns of the past, the Sufi acts in the world in a way that is most beneficial to the situation. Much of the initial work of the path is to enable the wayfarer to reach such a state of freedom, a freedom that does not follow the "oughts" and "shoulds" and other value judgments that imprison most people.

How many times have I heard someone deny her natural response to a situation with the attitude that she "should" do something else? So often people deny their heart in favor of conditioned values imposed by parents or society. The path painfully frees us from imposed restrictions, clears an inner space so that we can respond naturally. Khidr is not an abstract mystical figure, but an archetype of something essential within us. "The green one" images a natural aspect of our own divinity, something so ordinary that we overlook it. To follow the way of Khidr is to awaken to our own natural way of being with God and with life. In this natural state of being we know how to respond to the real need of the moment.

Nature does not think of the past or the future, but lives in the intensity of the moment. This moment contains the future, but does not limit it, as the caterpillar turning into a butterfly points to mystery and beauty beyond our rational expectations. We have within us a way of being that connects with the divine in each moment, that sings His song of praise with every breath. The mystical journey takes us back to this creative core of divine life that embraces the two worlds. In this core we are at the place where the two seas meet, where something within us is so dynamically alive that it cannot be constricted by past patterns. The mystical journey is an awakening and an unlearning, opening a door to a state of freedom that is always present but rarely lived.

Moses could not give up his rational self, his conditioned responses, and so had to part ways with Khidr. Moses could not live in the moment. How do we free ourself from the Moses within us, the aspect of ourself that always wants to do "the right thing," and so misses the real opportunity? How can we surrender to the way of Khidr that seems so contrary to our values and expectations? Khidr's final words to Moses provide the answer: "What I did was not by my own will. That is the meaning of my acts which you could not bear to watch with patience." The mystic follows the will of God, and His will is not written or learnt, but is accessible only in the moment. On the mystical path we have to both surrender our own will and catch the divine hint that belongs to the moment. We have to clear away the debris of our own self and become attuned to the timeless moment of the soul.

The energy of the path and the potency of our aspiration help to free us from ourself. The power of love breaks up our conditioning and confronts us with the patterns that imprison us. Our rational self is subtly subverted from within, while the grip of the mind is dissolved through meditation. And there is a simple technique which mystics have always used to bring us into the moment: awareness of the breath.

THE BREATH

In Persian, the language of Rûmî and many other Sufi writings, the word for breath and moment is the same, "*dam.*" Awareness of the breath is a practice that belongs to many spiritual traditions, and is often an integral part of a *mantra* or *dhikr.* In the *dhikr* Allâh described earlier (pp. 28–32), the repetition of His name is performed with the breath. Thus each time we repeat Allâh we are conscious of our own breath, of the cycle of out-breath to in-breath, and just as important, the moment between the in-breath and the out-breath. An awareness of this moment carries the greatest significance, for this is the moment when the soul returns to its own plane of existence. Repeating His name with an awareness of the breath, we consciously commune with the timeless moment of the soul.

With each cycle of the breath we make a conscious connection with the inner world. Our breath is a cycle that flows between the two worlds, the inner plane of pure being and the outer plane of physical reality. As we breathe out, the energy of life (*prana* in Sanskrit) flows from the inner plane into manifestation. With each in-breath this energy returns to its place of origin. The work of the wayfarer is to bridge the two worlds, to connect the inner and outer planes. The simple practice of awareness of the breath takes our consciousness from the inner to the outer world and then back to the inner. With each cycle of the breath we consciously participate with the flow of creation, with the primal dynamic of all life as it comes from the source into the outer world of forms, and then returns to its origin.

Moving between the two worlds, we become free from the prison of forms and become aware of the flow of life. Connecting with our inner self with every breath, we develop a life in which the outer is founded upon the inner. With each breath we return to the core of ourself and the source of our life. Our outer life ceases to become crystallized, cut off from its origin. Instead of a life founded upon the past, upon patterns built up over time, our life is nourished from within and we feel the primal joy of life lived from the source.

Being aware of our breath, of the cycle of out-breath and in-breath, is a powerful spiritual practice. "Awareness in the breath" or "awareness in the moment" (*Hush dar dam*) is the first of the eleven principles of the Naqshbandi Sufi path. The founder of this order, Bahâ ad-dîn Naqshband, said,

> The foundation of our work is in the breath. The more that one is able to be conscious of one's breathing, the stronger is one's inner life. It is a must for everyone to safeguard his breath in the time of his inhalation and exhalation and further, to safeguard his breath in the interval between the inhalation and exhalation.

As the wayfarer becomes occupied with the exercise of the moment (i.e. remembering the breath), he turns his attention from remembering the past and thinking of the future, and focuses on each breath until it is expired. In this way awareness of the breath takes us from the prison of time into the timeless dimension of our real self.

Becoming conscious of our breath makes us aware of our inner self which belongs only to the moment. We gradually move from a consciousness dominated by the concerns of the past and future, to a consciousness of the eternal present. We are awakened to a dimension of our self that is not caught in the illusion of time, but founded upon Reality. In the words of the Naqshbandi master al-Kashghari, "Awareness in the breath is moving from breath to breath so that there is no heedlessness but rather there is presence, and with each breath that we take there should be the remembrance of the Real."

THE WONDER OF THE MOMENT

Awareness of the breath turns our attention inward, helping us to become aware of what we have forgotten: the timeless present. Children live naturally in this reality, though we sadly forget it as we grow into adolescence. My own children reintroduced me to the magic of the present, as a simple walk to the corner shops became an endless adventure, with each puddle an ocean to be crossed, each stick a potential treasure to be picked up and inspected. I sensed the freedom of their experience, and how I was so much caught in the mind and its concerns of past and future.

My children lived in a wonder that seemed denied to me, though there had been times when I sensed this numinous quality of life. When I was seventeen I lived and worked on a small tropical island in New Guinea, where the environment was both primitive and breathtakingly beautiful, with enormous multicolored butterflies and parrots screeching from trees. I was very much alone and for the first time in my life there was little mental stimulus, no television, radio, books, or conversation; just the simplicity of waking before dawn and working on a coconut plantation. Slowly as the days passed my mind emptied until there was nothing to think about, and I could experience the pure beauty of the moment—a spider's thread shining in the soft dawn sunlight, a luminous snake slithering across the path, the moonlight caught in the water.

In this inner and outer landscape there was the simplicity of life that just *is*. During this time I wrote many haiku-like poems, trying to capture the precious simplicity of these moments: little fish bouncing on the water beside my canoe, a leaf dropping from palm trees, a child walking shielded from the rain by a banana leaf. I had been awakened to something I could not name, to something that seemed to have been so absent from my own childhood. For a few months after leaving this island and traveling in the Far East, I kept the sense of this presence. As I watched monks hanging their orange robes to dry in the sunshine, or smelled food cooked on a wok in the street, a moment was alive within me, precious and potent.

But when I returned to the West I found myself bombarded by so many mental images, so much information, so many cares and concerns, that I lost this essence. It could reappear unexpectedly when I would take a walk in the early dawn, or see snow fall on city streets bringing a sense of hush. But when I saw how my children naturally lived in the fullness of what is now, I felt a sense of regret and exclusion. Maybe we all forget this timeless time of childhood, as Wordsworth says: "The prison walls close round the growing boy." Maybe we remain with a sense of betrayal, or a sad acceptance of what we have lost. I personally have few memories of my childhood. As happens with many others, early innocence was quickly obscured by psychological pain. But the moments that became alive on a tropical island, and that I saw, almost jealously, in my own children, have reappeared in a different way through the practices of the path. Now these moments are no longer fleeting, and are accompanied by a profound sense of freedom.

THE PRACTICES OF THE PATH

Through meditation the mind becomes stilled, so that we are no longer a prisoner of its past and future thought-forms. Whether the mind is stilled for a minute or an hour does not matter, because without the mind there is no time, there is only the moment, whose time-less quality opens us to the infinite. "There is no dimension of time in God's world" and in the silence beyond the mind we glimpse this deeper reality. We step out of the known world governed by our preconceptions, our psychological and mental patterns, into a formless dimension that belongs only to God. In this dynamic silence we are naturally attuned to the ways of Khidr, to the direct perception of the heart.

Sufi meditation stills the mind and awakens the heart. The spinning of the heart infuses us with love, which belongs only to the infinite present. In love there is no time, as all lovers know who have tasted this tender and all-embracing substance. E. E. Cummings poignantly writes of lovers,

> how fortunate are you and i,whose home
> is timelessness:we who have wandered down
> from fragrant mountains of eternal now

In the moment of love you are in love forever, and would give yourself again and again. In human relationships this can create problems when you awaken from this embrace to discover the personal incompatibilities of the partner with whom you have felt this eternal moment. Coming back into the dimension of time and the concerns of the mind and psyche, you may feel that you have been bewitched by love's irrational power. But for the mystical lover there are no such complications. The mind may try to deceive you, make you doubt the wonder you have tasted, but once you have tasted the "wine that was before the creation of the vine," you gladly give yourself again and again.

Meditation awakens us to what is always present, love's eternal now. This love may fill us with bliss, saturate us with longing, touch us with silence, or just open a door to emptiness. Divine love has many qualities, and in our own individual way we "step out of the circle of time and into the circle of love." Coming out of meditation we are thrown back into the mind and a world only too often governed by time, but we bring with us a subtle knowledge of a different way of being. Slowly, over the years, this inner knowing of a place within us where time is not becomes like an invisible foundation to our consciousness, so that even in the midst of everyday activities we sense this other dimension.

Our Western world is very constricted by time—it is one of the prices we pay for a culture that values the mind to such a degree. Anyone who has been to India or the Far East has experienced a different attitude. I remember once on a small island in the Philippines waiting a week for a boat. Each day I would come to the dock with other passengers to see if the boat had come. But because the weather was stormy the boat did not arrive, and so we all waited another day, and no one seemed bothered or worried by the delay. In the West we have been conditioned to such a degree that we are demonized by time, always rushing or worrying if we are wasting time. To wait a week for a boat seems an abhorrence. We run our lives by schedules and have long forgotten that time is just a mental construct. Meditation gradually frees us from these chains, and even when we are outwardly constricted by a "tight schedule" we sense an inner freedom, and can pause for an instant to dip into the infinite expanses of the moment.

Meditation inwardly opens us, and the *dhikr* gives us a continual remembrance. With each and every breath we attune ourself to our Beloved, we connect with the dimension of the soul. At the beginning we can only practice the *dhikr* when our mind is not otherwise occupied, but part of its potency is how it goes into the unconscious where it repeats itself with the cycle of our breath. Like meditation it provides an inner foundation, a living connection to the eternal present. Constant remembrance is a continual immersion in the purifying waters of His presence as each and every breath becomes alive with His name.

These simple and ancient practices effortlessly align us. They were designed centuries ago by the masters of the path to change the structure of consciousness. The silent *dhikr* as practiced by the Naqshbandi Sufis was, according to tradition, taught by Khidr. Most Sufis practice a vocal, or loud *dhikr*, but when 'Abd'l-Khâliq al-Ghujduwânî, the first master of this path, was studying in Bukhara, he came across the Qur'anic verse (7:55), "Call upon your Lord in supplication and hiddenness." He was unable to discover its interpretation until Khidr appeared to instruct him in the method of the silent *dhikr*. Khidr caused him to repeat the divine name three times while submerged in water, which has both a practical and a symbolic significance.

The practices of the path enable us to live in the outer world while inwardly attuned to the inner reality of the heart. We learn to live at the place where the two seas meet, where the infinite world of the soul touches the temporal world of everyday life. Something within us becomes alive and swims free. We meet Khidr, the archetype of our own direct perception. And if we are able to avoid the limitations of Moses we can follow Khidr. Surrendering to what is beyond our understanding, we can unlearn our conditioning and be taught to act according to His will, according to the need of the moment.

What happens within the heart is always the greatest mystery, but sometimes we glimpse the wonder of how love draws us, how we are touched and taken by the divine. One friend was allowed in a dream to experience a little of her soul's love affair, and how through the breath she merged into the timeless moment of His love:

> Someone comes from behind and presses softly his lips onto my back, in the middle between my shoulders. It is like entering at my neck and hitting me at the heart, from behind. Incredible tenderness, love, and deepness are filling me, and immediately I know that I want to surrender to this kiss, not caring about what's happening around. Giving myself to it completely I notice that silence, complete silence, is filling the room, no sound, no movement, total stillness. Then I feel myself breathing, feel all the tenderness and love in my breath, and realize that it is through the breath that we are becoming one. My breathing is his breathing and his breathing is mine. We are one.
>
> This wonderful, blissful, and ecstatic experience lasts for a long and timeless moment, and then it's me, unfortunately, who separates again.

10. THE VEILS OF GOD
PART I

We are veiled from Thee only through Thee.

Ibn 'Arabî

EVERYTHING IS HE

The Sufi path draws us into the closed circle of love, to the intimacies of the heart and the unveiling of oneness. "The world is no more than the Beloved's single face," writes the poet Ghalib, and within the heart this secret is revealed. The veils of separation are drawn back so that the mystic can see with the eye of oneness, the single eye of the heart that sees the true nature of creation. The mutiplicity of life, the wonder of its myriad forms, is an embodiment of a oneness that reflects His oneness.

The mystical path is a process of unveiling. Often at the beginning of the journey we are given an experience of His oneness. For an instant the veils between the two worlds are lifted and we glimpse the underlying unity. This happened to me when I was sixteen and I read a Zen *koan* which opened a door that I never knew existed. For two weeks I laughed with joy at the wonder of life. I was at boarding school outside London, and after my schoolwork was over I would sit in a garden beside the river Thames, watching the flowing water as it headed towards a weir, and the branches of a willow tree dancing in reflection. It was early summer and the sunlight would sparkle, caught in the eddies of the current. There was a silence and peace I had never before experienced. I was full of unexplained joy, sensing that a secret had been revealed. Of course such states do not last. The veils between the worlds closed even more fully and I was thrown back into this world of isolation.

The doorway into life's real wonder had been opened and then closed, and I was left with an awareness of loss. The pain of consciousness reminds us that we are separate from oneness. We become like the reed torn from the reed bed, whose music is full of longing for the source. We long to go Home, back to where we belong, and this longing takes us on the most mysterious and demanding of journeys, the pilgrimage of the soul. On this journey the world that most people call their home becomes a painful place of separation, a world of illusion in which the face of our Beloved is veiled.

And yet, at the same time there is the hidden secret that this world is also God. Everything is He. The beauty of the world is a reflection of His beauty. Like sunlight reflected in a dewdrop, His light catches our attention. We sense that there is something behind the forms of this world. In the quiet of an early morning, or even amidst the clamor of city streets, a moment may remind us of this luminous presence; a piece of music or a heartfelt poem may touch this hidden chord. Like a stranger's face suddenly reminding us of a past lover, moments like these awaken feelings of love and longing. Once the door in the soul has been opened we are always at the mercy of strange moods of remembrance, as what the Sufis call the "fragrance from the garden of oneness" slips through the defenses of the mind and ego.

We are here amidst the many forms of life, sensing that our Beloved is elsewhere, and yet, paradoxically, knowing that He is always present. His world hides and reveals His face, and we are a part of this mystery. "Man is My secret and I am his secret," because man holds the secret of His creation, the wonder of unity and multiplicity. The many forms of life reflect His oneness, and man holds in his heart the mirror in which this mystical unveiling takes place. As the mystic journeys homeward, polishing the mirror of the heart with his devotion and aspiration, so the veils become more and more transparent. Then the secret hidden within the heart becomes part of our being, part of our life, until we can witness the truth expressed by Ibn 'Arabî:

> The existence of the beggar is His existence and the existence of the sick is His existence. Now when this is admitted, it is acknowledged that this existence is His existence and that the existence of all created things is His existence, and when the secret of one particle of the atom is clear, the secret of all created things, both outward and inward, is clear, you do not see in this world or the next, anything except God.

SEVENTY VEILS OF LIGHT AND DARKNESS

The path of lovers seeking their Beloved winds through the maze of the world. We sense His presence, and yet He is hidden. His veils keep us from Him and yet also protect us from the devastating power of His presence, from the blinding fierceness of His light. His creation is a veil of protection, as expressed in the *hadîth*, "God has seventy veils of light and darkness; were they to be removed the Glories of His Face would burn away everything perceived by the sight of His creatures." Although He is so near to us—"closer than the tear that runs between the eye and the eye-lid"—He shields us from the overwhelming intensity of His nearness. He protects us from Himself with His creation. Yet the mystic longs to lift these veils of illusion, to see behind the dance of creation.

The veils of separation are also the veils of protection. When just a few of these veils are lifted, the mind and ego are thrown in confusion, even despair. We glimpse a brightness that can easily blind us, a quality of love that can devastate us. If it is dangerous to look with the naked eye at the physical sun, how much more dangerous to be exposed to the Sun of suns, to that tremendous power and energy of which the physical sun is just a reflection.

A friend had a dream in which her sheikh stood in front of her with veils hanging from his arms. He told her that if he were to lift these veils for just a moment the brilliance of the light would make her mad. Then he pointed out a long and dusty road which she should walk. There is a reason that the mystical path is long and that patience is one of the most important qualities needed for the journey. We have to be gradually prepared to experience even a slight lifting of the veils. Through meditation and inner work we create a container of consciousness that enables us to experience the wonder of His oneness, the intensity of His presence, without having our everyday consciousness destroyed. Ego consciousness is so fragile, and is designed for this world of shadows, for this dimension of duality. It cannot contain a dimension of light upon light, love upon love, a oneness in which there is no semblance of duality.

We long for the world of light, for the oneness of love, for the company of our heart's Beloved. Yet the power of His presence overwhelms us, and can easily shatter our frail ego and mind. The Sufi says just to touch the hem of the garment of love throws the mind into confusion, bewilderment, even madness. Saʻdî tells a story of a young man who fainted just by seeing the dust raised by the dress of his beloved:

> A dervish appeared among one of the Bedouin tribes. A young man offered him a meal. While the young man was serving the dervish, he fell down and fainted. The dervish asked the others who were there why he had fainted and they said, "He has fallen passionately in love with his cousin. While she was moving in her tent, the young man glimpsed the dust raised by the train of her dress and fainted."
>
> The dervish went to the girl's tent and said, "I would like to intercede for the young man. Show him your favor! His love for you is so great!"
>
> The girl smiled. "He cannot stand glimpsing even the train of my dress. How do you imagine he could live in my presence?"

Saʻdî is not just telling a lover's tale. The "young man" symbolizes one who has not yet matured in the ways of divine love, who has not yet walked the dusty path. This is a realistic warning about the danger of divine presence to one who is unprepared. Once a woman came to a workshop I was giving in New York. There were only a few people present and there was time for her to tell her whole story. Years before she had had a powerful mystical experience of divine oneness in which everything, even the dog shit on the sidewalk, was divine, was an aspect of God and filled with His light. But she was unprepared for such an experience. She did not know what was happening and her mind, which knew only experiences of duality, was thrown into confusion. How can the ego exist when everything is one? What sense of ordinary reality can one have when one sees everything as God? Her mind could not cope and she went to a doctor who diagnosed her as manic-depressive, gave her electric shock treatment and then prescribed powerful anti-depressants. These drugs dulled her sensitivity and cut her off from her higher consciousness. By the time I met her, about four or five years later, she had been conditioned to believe that she was manic-depressive. I tried to convince her otherwise, but the doctors and drugs had had their effect.

The mystical path is a gradual process of preparation so that the wayfarer can become acclimatized to different levels of reality and still function in the everyday world. Over the years meditation prepares us for a dimension of oneness in which the ego does not exist, in which we are not. And we are able to come out of these states and return to the ego and continue our daily life. We learn to be a part of oneness and yet also a separate human being. We are opened to the beyond and yet able to remain here, with our feet on the ground in a world we know to be an illusion.

Mystical love is an experience of tremendous power. Most people experience love in a diluted form reflected in another human being. Love is then experienced as affection, caring, a quality of understanding in which we are held and supported. Only in the moment of sexual orgasm is there a glimpse of a different quality of love, as a power that throws us out of ourself. In these moments there is no partner, no other person, and at times not even ourself. This is the nature of mystical love, of the ecstasy that grips the lover. But mystical experiences are more pure and potent than sexual orgasm. They grip our whole being and are not limited to one or two moments.

The power of love throws us out of ourself as it drenches us in bliss. It is like being plugged into an energy source, and can be as exhausting as it is exhilarating. The experience can leave you gasping, wondering how much more ecstasy you can bear. Then the bliss that has gripped you is gone, leaving the body shaking and cold. The mind is left reeling, thrown upside down, while the ego is just dazed. There is a reason that Sufis are called drunkards, and the place of their intoxication "the tavern of ruin."

THE TAVERN OF RUIN

Once divine love has taken hold of a human being she is as if haunted, addicted, lost to herself. She is in the grip of the greatest power in the universe, a power that does not know the limitations of time or space. Pure love comes from the beyond and takes us into the depths of ourself where we encounter the nothingness of our true being. This is the path of annihilation in which we leave behind any semblance of ourself. The Sufis often speak of the danger of just one sip of this intoxicating wine, as in a poem by Shabistarî:

> The aroma of the Divine Wine
> Has made them abandon everything;
> The taste for Annihilation
> Has sent them all sprawling like drunkards.
> For one sip of the wine of ecstasy

They have thrown away pilgrim staff, water jar
   and rosary.
They fall, and then they rise again,
Sometimes bright in union,
Sometimes lost in the pain of separation;
Now pouring tears of blood,
Now raised to a world of bliss....

They have drunk one cup of the pure wine
And have become—at last, at long last—real Sufis.

The wine of love takes us behind the veils of creation, from a world of forms into a formlessness where we do not exist: where the lover is lost in the ocean of love. For the mystic there is "nothing but nothingness" and yet this nothingness loves us with a tenderness beyond imagining, with intimacy as well as devastating power. In the tavern of ruin we gladly lose everything we considered of value:

Drunk on the wine of selflessness,
They have given up good and evil alike.
Drunk, without lips or mouth, on Truth
They have thrown away all thoughts of name
   and fame,
All talk of wonder, visions, spiritual states,
Dreams, secret rooms, lights, miracles.

"Everything has to go" and everything is lost when love takes hold of a heart. This is not a path for the fainthearted, for those who like security or even the comfort of what is known. There is a place where the mystic and even the spiritual seeker must part, as I was shown in a vision when I saw a coffin on which was engraved "spiritual aspirant." The spiritual aspirant seeks a spiritual life, based upon some spiritual concept, some idea of how things ought to be. The mystic is drawn into the abyss of love, into the nothingness beyond any notion, "the dark silence in which all lovers lose themselves."

Few wayfarers realize that "everything has to go" actually means everything, every concept, every idea, every belief system. Every identity we have of ourself is swept away in the mad currents of love, in its dark abyss. All images of both God and self are dissolved and the mind is left helpless, the ego bewildered. The mystic is drawn into this vortex by a secret quality of her being that calls her to nothingness, that is attracted only by emptiness, by the essential nature of her own non-being.

Stamped within the heart of the lover is the knowledge that every form is a limitation. The Sufis say "In the name of He who has no name" because they know that only the nothingness is real. The innermost song of the mystic is this song of nothingness, of His essential non-being. His lovers stand on the edge of the world knowing the darkness that is love's infinite ocean. This is the darkness that carries the secret seed of life, but cannot be contained by any form.

THE ABYSS OF NON-BEING

The mystical path draws us to this abyss. At the beginning the nothingness can be frightening. Even though it calls us it can be terrifying. Soon after he came to the path one friend had the following experience in meditation:

> I am standing on a rock. The rock is surrounded
> by emptiness. A wind is howling around me
> and I know that the next step is to jump off the
> rock into the emptiness.

This experience was so frightening that he tried to forget it for many years. Only later did he realize that it was a foretaste of truth. The mystical path is a gradual awakening to this reality.

Slowly through years of meditation and spiritual practice the wayfarer comes to the edge of himself, to the borderland where only those who are lost venture. For some this nothingness evokes fear, while for others it may carry a strange familiarity. I always found that the emptiness was wonderfully reassuring, affirming something within me that is not limited. The nothingness carries a quality of something eternally real and uncontaminated by the burden of ego. I felt it when I first began to meditate in my teenage years, the affirmation of something beyond the mind, of an emptiness in which I felt I really belonged.

At the time I did not question or even think about these experiences. I had read about the Buddhist void and found this reality present. In this endless emptiness there is no personal God, no benevolent or caring creator. There is no image in which to encase any belief, just a sense of dynamic permanence, a stability that is beyond anything the outer world can offer. Closing my eyes I found this dimension at the borders of my mind and knew that I had found where I really belonged. I could let go of the clothes of being a person that seemed to carry so much weight and distress. I could relax in the deepest and most profound sense, like slipping into the warm waters of a tropical sea.

While this world had for me always seemed to present so much struggle, effort, and limitation, the emptiness took away every covering, even my isolated sense of self. Something essential was allowed to be. And it remains, always at the borders of consciousness. Of course I came out of those early experiences back into an everyday life that presented me with all of the intensity of growing up, the way life grips us in its dance of pleasure and pain, exploration and anticipation, hopes and fears. But whenever I really needed it the emptiness was present, without sentimentality, like a friend who knows the core of one's being, who is the core of one's being.

In the mystical emptiness there is no revelation, because there is no one there. In this dark silence can be no flash of "enlightenment," because "we" are not present. His presence can only be understood as a state of total absence. The mystical truth is that there is neither lover nor Beloved, neither creation nor Creator. The void is the startling reality that every mystic must encounter. Underlying creation is an astounding emptiness, darker than the space between the stars. All images of God are dissolved. There is only an ever-expanding nothingness which throws the mind and ego into a state of confusion near to madness. Who or what is revealed? Who or what is hidden in this revelation?

Turning inward, we turn away from the many towards the one, to the single source of our being. But we find no benevolent Creator, no caring or merciful God. We are lost in a state of non-existence that is beyond being. In this emptiness there is no revelation because there is no one present. His Presence can only be understood as a state of total absence, as illustrated by the story of al-Hallâj when he was in jail awaiting execution:

On the first night of his imprisonment the jailers came to his cell but could not find him in the prison. They searched through all the prison, but could not discover a soul. On the second night they found neither him nor the prison, for all their hunting. On the third night they discovered him in the prison.

"Where were you on the first night, and where were you and the prison on the second night?" they demanded. "Now you have both reappeared. What phenomenon is this?"

"On the first night," he replied, "I was in the Presence, therefore I was not here. On the second night the Presence was here, so that both of us were absent. On the third night I was sent back, that the Law might be preserved. Come and do your work."

On the first night al-Hallâj was with God, so he was absent. On the second night the Absolute Nothingness was present with him, so neither he nor the jail existed. On the third night he made the tremendous sacrifice: he surrendered to separation, to the mystery of incarnation in which we are separated from the One to Whom we belong. Al-Hallâj returned to the jail to be crucified for love. He welcomed his execution because he knew that death leads to the final union of the lover and the Beloved. On the gallows he paid the ultimate price to make public the secret of mystical oneness long known to the Sufis. Before the flagellation that preceded his execution he said:

Kill me, O my faithful friends
    for to kill me is to make me live;
My life is my death, and my death is my life.

The mystical paradox of union with God is that the lover is never present: "the Beloved is living, the lover is dead." In order to experience our Beloved, we are taken into the nothingness where we do not exist. In our Western culture we are so identified with our own self that of necessity we project our ego onto the path. We see the journey as leading to *our* experience of God, *our* realization of the Self. It is almost impossible to understand that the journey is not about us, that all our effort, sacrifice and suffering do not lead our own self anywhere, do not give *us* the longed-for mystical experience. Every notion of spiritual attainment is an illusion that has to be left behind; and it is often much more difficult to leave behind a spiritual illusion than a worldly illusion. When we have the desire for a new sports car we can easily recognize that is an illusion; the desire for a spiritual experience, or even to help others along the path, can be far more deceptive.

On the path of love the traveler and all of his expectations are left behind, as Rûmî writes: "There is no dervish, or if there is a dervish that dervish is not there." The Sufi master Bhai Sahib said, "People ask me: have you realized God? Have you realized the Self? I have not realized the Self. I have not realized God, I answer." Irina Tweedie, who knew he was a great sheikh, laughed, "Bhai Sahib, this is a lie!" But he replied:

> Why a lie? If I am nowhere, how can I realize something? To realize something there must be somebody to realize: if I am nothing, if I am nowhere, how can I have realized something?

Experience of God cannot be reported because there is no one there. The mind, the ego, and all faculties of consciousness are left behind. Bâyezîd Bistâmî came close to describing this state when he said that the third time he entered the Holy House he saw neither the House nor the Lord of the House, by which he meant, "I became lost in God, so that I knew nothing. Had I seen at all I would have seen God." 'Attâr, telling this story, adds the following anecdote:

> A man came to the door of Bâyezîd and called out.
> "Whom are you seeking?" asked Bâyezîd.
> "Bâyezîd," replied the man.
> "Poor wretch!" said Bâyezîd. "I have been seeking Bâyezîd for thirty years, and cannot find any trace or token of him."
> This remark was reported to Dhû'l-Nûn. He commented, "God have mercy on my brother Bâyezîd! He is lost with the company of those who are lost in God."

The mystical path prepares us for the shattering freedom of our own non-existence. In these moments we are lost, completely and utterly. Returning from beyond the mind we are left with a residue of the soul's experience. We glimpse the vast emptiness that lies beyond our seeming existence. The knowledge of our own non-being permeates into consciousness, reflected from a different dimension. Bâyezîd, speaking with the certainty of one who has been "lost in God" for "thirty years," knew the truth of his own non-existence. The mystical path is a gradual awakening to this reality. Slowly we come to know that we are not.

RETURNING FROM BEYOND THE EGO

Meditation is an important technique to enable us to transcend the ego and the mind. Stilling the mind, we begin to have access to a different dimension. Initially we feel the invisible presence and effect of the beyond. But as our meditation deepens we can develop a consciousness of what is beyond the ego. Then we come to *know* the illusory nature of the ego. Going into meditation I have had the experience of leaving the ego and then *seeing* my own ego-consciousness as a separate entity like a small planet in space, a planet which seemed two-dimensional. Experiencing the vastness of space and the expansion of my true being, I saw how the ego was quite separate and self-enclosed, a world unto itself. I knew that I was not my ego, could never be my ego. Ego-consciousness looked so limited, defined by such a small parameter compared to the vastness of inner space which was the home of my real being.

As the inner experience became deeper and richer I left the ego far behind. Then I entered a darkness in which all consciousness, all sense of self, was lost. But then, coming back out of meditation, I felt myself returning, as if from far away, to this "planet," this small, constricting identity we call the ego. I felt myself slipping into ego-consciousness as one would slip into an old suit of clothes. I was aware that once again I was "becoming" this familiar identity with its self-image, its mental patterns, its limited horizon. I saw how easily the ego blocked my experience of a deeper reality, drew a curtain over the vastness of my inner being. I experienced both the constriction and the comfort of this familiar self, this "I." Finally, fully awaking out of meditation, I was back in the ego, with the knowledge of the experience just at the borders of consciousness.

Such experiences free us from the grip of the ego. How can the ego rule us when we know that it does not exist? Initially when we come back from meditation the mind cuts us off from the inner experience. This is necessary; otherwise we could easily become unbalanced by being confronted by our own non-existence. But slowly this deeper reality infuses itself, and becomes liberating rather than shattering. There is a deep freedom in knowing one's non-existence.

As we progress along the path we develop a psychological strength and quality of consciousness that can contain these very different realities: our everyday ego-self and a deeper dimension that is featureless and formless, unlimited and undefined. We are freed from the prison of our ego-self and yet still able to function in an outer reality that requires that we think we exist as a separate person. The wayfarer who has been lost in love, who has tasted the truth of her non-existence, becomes a "soldier of two worlds." She learns to be immersed in the shoreless seas of love and also participate fully in an outer life with its many demands.

Through meditation we develop a quality of consciousness that is not bound by the ego and the ordinary mind. In meditation we are able to become conscious "somewhere else," and then even this higher consciousness dissolves in the mystical darkness as we are lost to all sense of self, as we dissolve in a dimension where we are not. But waking from meditation, we no longer completely cut off this experience. The "higher mind" enables us to bring back an awareness of this other reality—although initially it can be very confusing to experience these different realities, as the poet Fakhruddîn 'Irâqî poignantly expresses:

If You are Everything
   then who are all these people?
And if I am nothing
   what's all this noise about?
You are Totality,
   everything is You. Agreed.
Then that which is "other-than-You"—
   what is it?
Oh, indeed I know:
   Nothing exists but You:
but tell me:
   Whence this confusion?

Existence and non-existence, multiplicity and oneness: which is real and which is illusion? How can there be any illusion when everything is He? When He has revealed Himself, who remains? What is the ego when there is consciousness of oneness? But gradually the confusion clears as the veils of separation become the veils of revelation. We can never know God: "None knows God but God." In His presence we do not exist. But as we glimpse the wonder of our non-existence and the ego loses its grip, so a transition takes place. The world that had hidden the face of our Beloved begins to reveal Him to us. No longer caught in the limited vision of the ego, the lover begins to see with the single eye of the heart.

When our consciousness is ruled by the ego, we see through the eyes of the ego. We experience a world in which we are present and He is absent. The world seems a playground of illusions, or a desert filled only with our longing for Him. But when the ego surrenders its power, then the eye of the heart opens and reveals the hidden face of creation. The eye of the heart is an organ of spiritual consciousness that belongs to the

Self. Through this eye we see things as they really are, as a reflection of our Beloved. We cannot know Him in His essential non-being, but we come to know Him reflected in His creation. In the beauty of His forms we come to know His beauty. The world of multiplicity becomes a mirror in which we can see His oneness:

> In our hall of mirrors the map of one Face appears
> As the sun's splendor would spangle a world
>   made of dew.

11. THE VEILS OF GOD
PART II

Wheresoever you turn, there is the face of God.

Qur'an

THE EYE OF THE HEART

The path of love takes the lover behind the veils of creation into the ocean of love's oneness where all semblance of self dissolves. In this infinite ocean where "swimming ends always in drowning," the lover merges into the infinite emptiness that is at the core of creation. Love's truth is a vortex of nothingness out of which is born the dance of life, the opposites that spiral into manifestation. From the formless emptiness the multiplicity of forms comes into being. From the depths of His non-being He brings forth being, and each cell of creation has His name stamped in its center.

The mystic who has passed behind the veils of the world has tasted the truth of his own non-being. The lover who has been lost then returns, knowing his ego-self to be an illusory fragment. And although the mystic can never know God, in the moment of being lost and the moment of returning a secret is revealed. On the borders of nothingness the lover is infused with the knowledge of love's oneness: the heart of hearts awakens into the presence of its Beloved. The ego has surrendered, has bowed down before its Lord; the lower has merged into the higher. This is the moment of mystical revelation when we come to know what is hidden from creation.

The path takes us to this point, when the "smaller merges into the Greater." In the words of the Sufi master Bhai Sahib, "One day the self will go, then only love will remain.... You will not say: I love. Where will the 'I' be?" When the ego has been merged into the Self it ceases to be the dominant factor. A quality of being emerges from within the heart to become the focal point of life. This quality of being does not belong to the ego but to the Self. It is a reflection of His being: "God is, and nothing is with Him." Initially experienced in meditation or at the moment of emerging from meditation, the consciousness of being gradually becomes present in everyday life. This consciousness is the consciousness of divine presence, the consciousness of oneness which we carry with us in our daily life.

The mystical path always takes us by surprise as it reveals what has been hidden. I remember when I was drawn into this oneness of life. I had just moved from North London to the coast of California. After living for twenty years in the midst of a spiritual community with almost a hundred people coming to our house most days for meditation, I was alone with my family in a small coastal town. For days the telephone did not ring and no one knocked on our door. I spent my time writing, meditating, and walking. In the midst of this aloneness, nature opened her hidden self; the physical world became a part of my spiritual path in a way that I never expected. Among the trees and on the beaches I found a oneness revealing itself in the outer world.

That winter was a part of a six-year drought in California. In England I had been used to the months of January and February as being depressingly grey, wet, and dismal. Here it was warm and sunny. In January I would walk on the beach, alone in the sunshine. In February spring came, with wildflowers opening on the headlands. With the unexpected spring came this new consciousness. Suddenly I found, walking in the woods or beside the ocean, an overwhelming sense of oneness. In meditation I have at times glimpsed the oneness behind creation, the oneness that contains everything and mirrors His oneness. But now I was experiencing this oneness *in full consciousness*. Wherever I was walking, looking at the multiplicity of nature, the different leaves, trees, rocks washed by the waves, a oneness was visibly present. This oneness was so natural, so much a part of what I saw and felt. It had always been there, only now I was seeing it for the first time.

Nature revealed to me something so wonderful that I just looked in awe. The multiplicity was there, the tide-pools full of creatures, the hawks circling, the star-shaped flowers, but behind and around it was a permeating presence. At the beginning I was just fascinated, expecting this oneness to be a passing mystical state. But gradually I sensed its permanence. After writing for a few hours in the morning I would go for a walk, and looking, find it, both visible and intangible. I sensed and saw the oneness, but not with my physical eyes. An inner eye had opened in which place and state of being were united—the inner and outer oneness mirrored each other.

LOVE'S CERTAINTY

I had always experienced this world as a place of separation, and I longed for the beyond. Meditation had

taken me into an emptiness that felt familiar and reassuring. But the oneness that was revealed was beyond
any imagining, unexpected and wonderful. And it remains, always at the borders of consciousness, a sense
of presence in a world that before had only echoed with
absence. Something real is present in a world full of
illusions.

At the beginning these veils of illusion prevent us
from seeing our Beloved. Knowing this outer world is
not real, we seek what our restless heart longs for. We
are drawn by this primal need, to look within, to go
deeper and deeper, to return to the "root of the root of
our own self." But once we have touched the hem of
His garment, the ancient secret of lovers, then the path
transforms itself: the world of appearances stops being
a veil of separation and becomes a veil of revelation.
What had appeared an impenetrable wall of unreality
begins to be permeated with His divine light.

This transition is not a single moment of revelation. Like many processes it reflects the spiral nature
of the path in which we repeat a similar experience at
different levels of intensity, as we awaken more and
more fully to the higher consciousness of the Self.
At first imperceptibly, a quality of "being" is born within us through which we sense a reality hidden within
this world. There may be powerful experiences that
accompany this awakening, moments of illumination
or oneness, but often it is a gradual transition which
only later do we realize has taken place.

As our consciousness begins to change, as an
inner perception opens, the inner reality of oneness
begins to manifest through the outer world. This opening is different for each of us. Each wayfarer makes
his own journey behind the veils and then realizes within himself and within the world the qualities of his

Beloved. In His own unique way He reveals Himself to each of us, for, in the words of al-Makkî, "He never reveals Himself in a single form twice or in a single form to two individuals." Each traveler can only tell his own tale. On my own journey there were many years of turning inward. Each time I came to our meditation group I would retire to a corner in silence, not even understanding the need of other friends to talk. The conversation, dreams, and experiences of others passed me by. What was shared I cannot remember. There was within me instead a hunger, a need and despair that drove me inward. I noticed neither others nor how I was with others. Only later did I understand the importance of the community of friends, of talking, laughing, telling stories, of being together in companionship. I also realized that my behavior could have been seen as unbalanced and even rude in the disregard I had for others. However, the group had an understanding and tolerance that belong to those whose commitment is to the path. In fact each of us will at some time pass through a stage when we have no desire for outer communion, and may even positively dislike relating to fellow wayfarers.

But gradually a change happened within me and the focus of my attention was no longer turned so definitely away from the outer world. Possibly two experiences which I had in meditation were a significant part of this transition. One was the first time I consciously awoke somewhere else, to find myself in the presence of my teacher, who handed me a key. It was such a real experience that I was quite shocked when I came out of meditation to realize that I was in my teacher's meditation room, and all the time I had been meditating, my teacher had, on the physical plane, been in her kitchen next door talking and having tea with friends. When I told her of this experience she just said that it was "very auspicious" and that a key is an important symbol. Now I see this first experience of awakening on a different plane of consciousness as a turning point. In *consciously knowing* that I was not limited to every-day consciousness, I had been given a key to the door to the beyond.

The second important experience was of being loved totally and absolutely. I had just slipped off in meditation when I felt for a moment within my heart a love so complete that nothing more could be desired. From this gentlest touch, like butterfly wings around the edge of my heart, I knew the truth of Rûmî's words:

> subtle degrees
> of domination and servitude
> are what you know as love
>
> but love is different
> it arrives complete
> just there
> like the moon in the window.

Just an instant's touch within the heart and I *knew* that I was loved with a completeness that cannot be found in the outer world. The totality of the love included everything within me. This moment of love changed my life, in that I found the absolute security I had been seeking. I could now live without the insecurity that had haunted me. The outer world no longer carried the threat of incompleteness.

The first instance of His touch carries the beauty of a first love. Other experiences of His love have followed, deeper and more intoxicating. But in that moment everything was present and the foundation of my life in the world was changed.

These two experiences imprinted within my consciousness the knowledge of a freedom and wholeness that are not dependent upon the transient outer world. The hidden remembrance of the heart had been confirmed. Grounded within this absolute security, I was able to return to the world of forms with an affirmation of His presence within my consciousness. And because our experience of the outer world is a reflection of our state of consciousness, the outer world then began to reflect this inner reality. In the forms that had hidden Him I came to know His qualities.

THE FRAGRANCE OF HIS PRESENCE

Before, I had looked for Him unknowingly. I had sought His being in everything. In the early mornings I had walked among the fields as the sun infused the horizon with pink and then red. I had sensed something hidden in this beauty, in the cobwebs of dew spangled with sunlight. Sitting beside a stream I had watched the water tumble among the rocks and felt a stillness behind this movement, a peace in the swirling eddies of water. But I did not know Whom I looked for. Seeing His face reflected everywhere, I did not recognize it.

Falling in love, I felt the truth of Rûmî's words that

> a woman is God shining
> through subtle veils,

and like the firefly was drawn into the flames of Her beauty, the mystery of Her passion. I was intoxicated by the shimmering light of these veils, the tumbling locks of her hair and depth of her eyes. As in the imagery of Sufi poets, I was caught, entangled in the bewitching wonder of Her form:

> My heart on your tresses' twists
> Was caught, not just my heart,
> My soul too, in the same crux
> Became entangled.

Before, I had turned away from these forms, from these entanglements, from the reflection of His face. But now my heart was caught and I gladly gave myself. I allowed myself to be lost in a human love affair. I marveled at Her mystery, the feminine side of God that holds the intoxication of wonder. Yet through giving myself so completely to my heart's beloved, I gave myself to love itself. Love can never betray you. I knew that holding Her reflection would not fill the vacuum of my heart. I walked the blissfully painful path of human love with intoxication and tears, always knowing that love's essence was elsewhere, hidden and yet addictively present.

"The Prophet loved perfume, beautiful women and the shining of eyes in prayer." The fragrance of the Beloved can be found in many places. He comes to us through the mystery of His forms, through images which carry the secret of remembrance. To each of us He comes in our own way, according to our nature and temperament. Some see His face in the eyes of hungry children or in the need of the sick. For the artist He may make Himself known in the paintbrush or in the feel of wood. For some He is visible in nature, or in the wonders seen through a microscope.

We can never know His essence, His non-being, but through His creation we can sense His divine being. He is always present, "He is with you wherever you are," and when the ego loses its grip, we become open to experience His presence. We can see His wonder and beauty reflected in His world, come to know the qualities of our Beloved, what the Sufis call His names and attributes. When the eye of the heart opens, a world that had hidden Him begins to reflect these qualities. The mirror of creation that had before only shown us our own impermanent nature begins to reflect Him in whose image we are made. At first sparingly, and then with greater potency and frequency, we experience what the poet Gerard Manley Hopkins knew:

> The world is charged with the grandeur of God.
> It will flame out like shining from shook foil.

THE FOOTSTEPS OF THE BELOVED

"To meet you I look at face after face, appearance after appearance." The lover seeks for her Beloved, finding His imprint amidst the forms and images of His world. Part of the wonder of His unveiling is the way He comes to us through our own essential nature, in a way that is unexpected because it is so familiar. Although I have sensed His oneness in nature, honored His beauty in His creation, and felt the truth of Ibn 'Arabî's words that "Woman is the highest form of earthly beauty," for me dreams carry the most visible imprint of His presence. I have always been a lover of dreams. I remember at boarding school when the lights were turned off in the evening and other boys reached for their flashlights to read under the bedcovers, I was happy to fall asleep and enter the world of dreaming. Then dreams may have been just an escape from a mundane and imprisoning world. Later I would discover how some dreams are woven with a golden thread that connects us with our real nature.

Dreams embrace the images of the outer world and yet have a translucence that belongs to the beyond. In my own dreams I sensed His presence long before I consciously knew Him. Drawn into the practice of dreamwork, I found myself involved in the dreams of others, and here I found His footsteps most visible and came to know Him better.

There are many different types of dreams, and only some come from the spiritual dimension of our being. These dreams carry an atmosphere that belongs to our transcendent Self, which makes Itself felt in the telling of the dream. Through the dream a quality of the Beloved is reflected into consciousness. He has many different names and attributes, and different dreams reflect individual qualities. He may appear as the majestic beauty of a range of snow-capped mountains, or the subtle beauty of a flower. He can come with the power of a tremendous storm, or the absolute authority of the Self whose voice must be unquestioningly obeyed. He has the strength of an elephant and the lightness of a feather. Sometimes He comes with the sweetness and softness of a lover's touch, as in the following dream image:

> Suddenly a slim and delicately built woman appears, dressed in a simple orange-yellow robe. I take her in my arms, kiss her, and the taste is wonderfully sweet.
>
> I lie down with her and we melt into each other. Her body disappears in a second as a wave of sweetness, bliss, and peace pulsates like a wind through my whole being.

But the Beloved does not always appear as a tender lover bringing sweetness and bliss. There is an aspect of God that is overpowering and terrible; there is a potency of His love that overwhelms us. Sometimes the Beloved comes as an instinctual passion that grips us from the hidden recesses of our own soul. In the following dream this primal aspect of His power is imaged as a black panther:

> I am sitting in a bar at a city street corner, naked apart from a yellow half slip and black high heels. I am waiting for the black panther. I have a memory that he once penetrated me from behind. Because I do not know when he might be coming again I am always attentive, waiting. There is the feeling that when he comes, a tent appears over him; thus an intimate act can take place in a private place. I awake with the phrase, "Watch, for you know neither the day nor the hour when the bridegroom cometh." (*St. Matthew* 25:13)

This dream speaks of a love that comes from behind and penetrates us from the depths of the unconscious, from the unknown. This is no cerebral or idealized relationship, but an instinctual passion that overwhelms the lover and then leaves her, a victim of love, full of longing, waiting for whenever this unknowable, unexplainable potency will again take her. Once we have experienced this passion we remain always attentive, always waiting, knowing neither the day nor the hour when the bridegroom cometh.

One dreamer is taken by the sweetness of his Beloved, melting into an embrace of bliss and peace. For another He comes "like a thief in the night," while for another wayfarer the journey takes him to his teacher's house where he experiences the absolute darkness of God:

> I go to visit the teacher in her house, which in the dream is a makeshift Indian hut. I open the door. I know the teacher is at home, yet when I open the door there is no one there, nothing but darkness, a blackness more absolute than anything I have ever seen before. Apart from the darkness I am aware of an ominous wind. It blows in the house like a wind of change. I stand on the doorstep and feel afraid.

This wayfarer is taken beyond any human form or image, into a darkness where the wind of the spirit is present. The presence of the Beloved can evoke both intimacy and fear. He is soft and tender and forceful and violent. He also has the quality of aloneness which all wayfarers come to experience within themselves. The following dream evoked this aloneness, and brought a sense of desolation which is a human response to the absolute nature of His solitariness:

> I was floating in the sea after a shipwreck. At a distance from me were many other bodies also floating after the shipwreck. They were making no effort to swim and I knew that the current would not take them to shore. Eventually they would all drown. I was not making any effort to swim, but I was in a different current which slowly took me to the shore. When I came out of the water onto the shore I realized I was totally alone. Not just because I was the

only survivor, but there was no one else in the whole land. I felt totally and desolately alone.

The shipwreck of the ego leaves the dreamer in the current of the path. This current will take her to a different shore, the aloneness of the soul. In the words of al-Hallâj, "Solitary, God loves only the solitary—One, He loves only he who witnesses Him as One." In our aloneness we come to know His aloneness.

In listening to these dreams, one can hear the echoes of the footsteps of the Beloved walking across the hearts of His friends. The traceless path of love comes in many forms. He appears and reappears, glimpsed through the veils of the stories of love. Sometimes when a dream is told the room fills with the silence of His emptiness, or the joy of His kindness. There is laughter at the way He tricks us, how we are fooled by His cunning, diverted from the roads of reason by love's seduction. Or a dream full of longing will touch the hearts of those present, reminding us of the endless journey that is our commitment to Him.

THE SPIES OF GOD

As our focus shifts from the ego to the Self, so the Beloved comes to meet us. In dreams, in inner experiences, or in waking consciousness He reveals Himself according to our own nature. We are made in the image of God and deeper than our personality are our divine qualities. He comes to us in the clothes of our divine nature. Sometimes he comes with the tenderness of a lover's touch, or with the power of a whirlwind. Sometimes He disrupts our life, or brings unexpected harmony.

And always in this meeting are the threads of union, the secret oneness of lover and Beloved.

As we walk the long, dusty road, love empties us, pain purifies us, tears wash away our isolated self. Each time He comes to us there is more space for our Beloved; we intrude less and less upon this innermost meeting. In our longing and aspiration we journey Homeward, slowly emptying ourself of ourself. There is a saying much loved by the Sufis:

> My servant ceases not to draw nigh unto Me
> by works of devotion, until I love him, and
> when I love him I am the eye by which he sees
> and the ear by which he hears.

As our divine qualities come closer to consciousness we begin to experience life not just through the limited vision of the ego, but through the circle of the Self in which our divine nature is born. As our divine child opens its eyes the true nature of life is seen.

The Sufi is the servant of God, and our work is to be empty so that He can use us as He wills. Through the eyes of His servant He looks at His world, as is expressed in the beautiful image of Ibn 'Arabî, of the friend of God as "the pupil in the eye of humanity." Through the eye of the heart He looks at His world, which is why Sufis are sometimes called "the spies of God." Through our heart we look towards God and He looks towards the world. He needs us "to be here for Him." Mystical life is an acceptance of this simple duty of love and devotion. We remain here in this world of separation to serve Him.

Sufis are "a brotherhood of migrants who keep watch on the world and for the world." We are migrants because this is not a true home. We belong only to Him whom we love. When we have tasted the truth of our non-being, when we have lifted the veils of separation, we know that only He exists. We belong to Him since before the beginning of time. Returning from the states of non-existence, from meditation in which we are dissolved, lost in love, we put on the clothes of appearance in order to serve Him in His world. And serving Him we come to know Him, come to know how He reflects Himself in His world. We see how this world is a mirror in which the face of our Beloved is hidden.

The mystical journey is from separation back to union, and then returning from union to a state of servanthood. The first part of this journey is "the journey back to God" in which we turn our attention away from the veils of separation, seeking the truth that can only be found within the heart. The *shahâda, "Lâ ilâha illâ 'llâh"* (There is no god but God), describes this process of turning away from the illusion of the outer world where He is absent, *"Lâ ilâha"* (There is no god), towards the inner reality of the heart where He is present, *"illâ 'llâh"* (but God). Negating the outer world of forms, we affirm His formless inner presence.

But this work of negation and affirmation is only the first stage of the *shahâda*. The process of separation is followed by a deeper union which affirms that nothing is other than He: *"Lâ ilâha illâ 'llâh."* With each breath we affirm the union of the two worlds, and of our heart's Beloved who both hides and reveals Himself. In the words of Abû Sa'îd, "Sufism consists of keeping the heart from anything that is not He. But there is not anything not He."

The mystical path embraces the painful truth of separation and the deeper reality of love's union. When we return to the world from the mystical states of union, it may at first seem we return to the desert of separation. But having given ourself in service, we belong to our Beloved more completely. He who had abandoned us has never betrayed us. He who hid Himself from us did so only to reveal Himself more fully. The wonder of the world begins to shine with the light of our Beloved. The injustices, the suffering, the beauty, and the chaos remain. We still cry to Him for help, compassion, mercy. But in a wonderful and most mysterious way the oneness that had been hidden within the heart becomes a part of our everyday life.

The wayfarer who has traveled this ancient journey, who has been burnt in the fire of love's passion, is remade, reformed from the depths of the soul. Love takes us back to love; love reveals our innermost nature and takes us to where we belong. Once we have awakened to the oneness within the heart, we become immersed in this oneness more and more completely. The inner and outer worlds dance together, the song of the soul becomes the texture of our life, and the deepest meaning of being human resonates within us.

The mystical path never ends just as love never ends. The lover is drawn further and further into the oneness of the heart. Gradually the painful days of separation become just a memory, the desert of loneliness is left behind, and a wonder becomes more and more present. When the eye of the heart is opened, everything becomes a mirror for His face, everything a sign of His oneness. The lover who has tasted the truth of love knows that He is both the betrayer and the betrayed, both the maker and the dispeller of illusions. Every word has at its core the one word of His name. Every phrase is an act of praise. Everything rests in Him, and in the midst of life there is nothing other than Him:

"Whose beloved are You?"
    I asked,
"You who are so
    unbearably beautiful?"
"My own," He replied,
    "for I am one and alone
love, lover, and beloved
    mirror, beauty, eye."

BIBLIOGRAPHY

Abû Sa'îd ibn Abî-l-Khayr. *The Secret of God's Mystical Oneness.* Trans. John O'Kane. Costa Mesa, CA: Mazda Publishers, 1992.

Al-Qushayri. *Principles of Sufism.* Trans. B. B. Von Schlegell. Berkeley: Mizan Press, 1990.

Attâr, Farîd ud-Dîn. *The Conference of the Birds.* Trans. Afkham Darbandi and Dick Davis. London: Penguin Books, 1984.

Bhatnagar, R. S. *Dimensions of Classical Sufi Thought.* Delhi: Motilal Banarsidass, 1984.

Bowie, Fiona, ed. *Beguine Spirituality.* New York: Crossroad, 1990.

Chittick, William C. *The Sufi Path of Love.* Albany: State University of New York Press, 1983.

—. *The Sufi Path of Knowledge.* Albany: State University of New York Press, 1989.

Corbin, Henry. *The Man of Light in Iranian Sufism.* London: Shambhala Publications, 1978.

Cummings, E. E. *Selected Poems 1923–1958.* London: Faber and Faber, 1960.

—. *73 Poems.* London: Faber and Faber, 1974.

Fakhruddîn 'Irâqî, *Divine Flashes.* Trans. Wilson, Peter Lamborn. New York: Paulist Press, 1982.

Harvey, Andrew, *Light Upon Light,* Berkeley: North Atlantic Books, 1996.

—. *Perfume of the Desert,* Wheaton: Quest Books, 1999.

Holy Bible, Authorized Version. London: 1611.

Hopkins, Gerard Manley. *The Poems and Prose of Gerard Manley Hopkins.* Harmondsworth: Penguin Books, 1953.

Jung, C. G. *Collected Works.* London: Routledge & Kegan Paul.

Kingsley, Peter. "Knowing Beyond Knowing." In *Parabola* vol. xx no. 1, Spring 1997, pp. 21–24.

Massignon, Louis. *The Passion of al-Hallâj.* Princeton: Princeton University Press, 1982.

Mitchell, Stephen, ed. *The Enlightened Heart.* New York: Harper & Row, 1989.

—. trans. *Tao Te Ching.* New York: Harper & Row, 1988.

Nicholson, R.A. *Studies in Islamic Mysticism.* Cambridge: Cambridge University Press, 1921.

Nizami. *The Story of Layla & Majnun.* Trans. R. Gelpke. London: Bruno Cassirer, 1966.

Nurbakhsh, Javad. *Sufi Symbolism* Volumes I-IV. London: Khaniqahi Nimatullahi Publications, 1984-1990.

Power, Richard, ed. *Great Song: The Life and Teachings of Joe Miller.* Athens, GA: Maypop Books, 1993.

The Qur'an. Trans. M.H. Shakir. Elmhurst, New York: Tahrike Tarsile Qur'an, 1991.

Rûmî. *Rûmî, Poet and Mystic.* Trans. Nicholson, R. A. London: George Allen and Unwin, 1950.

—. *Rumi: Fragments, Ecstasies.* Trans. Liebert, Daniel. Santa Fe, NM: Source Books, 1981.

—. *Open Secret.* Trans. John Moyne and Coleman Barks. Putney, VT: Threshold Books, 1984.

—. *We Are Three.* Trans. Coleman Barks. Athens, GA: Maypop Books, 1987.

—. *Delicious Laughter.* Trans. Coleman Barks. Athens, GA: Maypop Books, 1990.

—. *Like This.* Trans. Coleman Barks. Athens, GA: Maypop Books, 1990.

—. *One-Handed Basket Weaving.* Trans. Coleman Barks. Athens, GA: Maypop Books, 1991.

—. *Birdsong.* Trans. Coleman Barks. Athens, GA: Maypop Books, 1993.

—. *The Essential Rumi.* Trans. Coleman Barks with John Moyne. New York: HarperCollins, 1995.

Scheeling, Andrew. *For Love of the Dark One: Songs of Mirabai.* Boston: Shambhala Publications, 1993.

Schimmel, Annemarie. *Mystical Dimensions of Islam.* Chapel Hill: University of North Carolina Press, 1975.

—. *I Am Wind, You Are Fire.* Boston: Shambhala Publications, 1992.

Scott Johnson, N. "Ocean and Pearls, Ibn Sab'în and the Doctrine of Absolute Unity", *Sufism,* Issue 25, Spring 1995. London: Khaniqahi Nimatullahi Publications.

Shabistarî. *The Secret Rose Garden.* Trans. Florence Lederer. Grand Rapids: Phanes Press, 1987.

Tweedie, Irina. *Daughter of Fire: A Diary of a Spiritual Training with a Sufi Master.* Point Reyes, CA: The Golden Sufi Center, 1986.

Vaughan-Lee, Llewellyn. *The Bond with the Beloved: The Mystical Relationship of the Lover and the Beloved.* Point Reyes, CA: The Golden Sufi Center, 1993.

—. *In the Company of Friends: Dreamwork within a Sufi Group.* Point Reyes, CA: The Golden Sufi Center, 1994.

—. *Sufism, the Transformation of the Heart.* Point Reyes, CA: The Golden Sufi Center, 1995.

—. *Catching the Thread: Sufism, Dreamwork, and Jungian Psychology.* Point Reyes, CA: The Golden Sufi Center, 1998.

—. ed. *Travelling the Path of Love: Sayings of Sufi Masters.* Point Reyes, CA: The Golden Sufi Center, 1995.

Vitray-Meyerovitch, Eva de. *Rûmî and Sufism.* Sausalito, CA: The Post-Apollo Press, 1987.

Wilson, Peter Lamborn and Pourjavady, Nasrollah. *The Drunken Universe.* Grand Rapids: Phanes Press, 1987.

Yeats, W. B., Trans. (with Shree Purohit Swami). *The Ten Principal Upanishads.* London: Faber and Faber, 1937.

GLOSSARY

Alif - first letter of the Arabic alphabet, symbolizing non-deviation and the unity of all opposites

anima - the feminine inner partner of a man; the inner woman of a man

animus - the masculine inner partner of a woman; the inner man of a woman

annihilation - (*fanâ*) dying to oneself in God; the burning away of the ego

archetype - the imprint of a specific god or goddess within the psyche; the energy of that imprint

arena - the inner circle of one's self where one is alone before God

baqâ - subsistence in God after the annihilation in Him; the journey in God

Beloved - the name by which mystics call God

conditioning - the psychological structure we have acquired in life from our families and society

dam - breath

dervish - refers to poverty, hence a Sufi wayfarer; member of a Sufi order

dhikr - mantra, repetition of a sacred phrase or name of God

eye, of the heart - the inner organ of consciousness. The heart has its own inner senses, sight, hearing, smell, etc.

fanâ - (annihilation) dying to oneself in God; the burning away of the ego

Friend - name given by Sufis to God, the Great Beloved

hadîth - traditions; sayings of the Prophet

hatha yoga - system of practices to raise the Divine energy through specific physical techniques

heart - that which contains the organ of spiritual consciousness

heart of hearts - innermost chamber of the heart, the hidden place belonging only to God

hint - a term referring to spiritual guidance given to a human being

homesickness - the longing for the true Home

Hush dar dam - watching or being conscious of each breath as a way to remember God

koan - riddle traditionally given to a disciple by a Zen teacher, designed to defeat the striving-mind and thus to throw the disciple beyond the mind into the Oneness which unites seeming opposites

Khidr - the "green one," the archetypal teacher figure in Sufism, the figure of direct revelation

Kun! - the command "Be!" of great esoteric meaning to the Sufi mystic, having to do with God's manifestation of Himself in Creation

longing - the pain of the heart's remembrance of God

mirror, of the heart - the aspect of the lover's heart which is polished until the Beloved can see His own face in it

muezzin - one who five times daily calls the faithful to prayer from the minaret of the mosque

nafs - the Sufi term for the lower nature of the human being

ney - the reed flute, the sound of which echoes the longing in the heart of a lover of God

numinous - radiating the energy of the Divine

opus contra naturam - the alchemist's "work against nature," where wholeness at one level is broken to allow transformation of energy onto a higher level

ouroboros - the world serpent which eats its own tail; the Great Wheel of Life

pole(s) - friend(s) of God around whom various aspects of the universe turn

polishing, of the heart - traditional term for inner work, cleaning of the heart

poverty, of the heart - a state of inner attachment to God and freedom from outer attachments

Primordial Covenant - the moment when God asks the not-yet-created humanity, "Am I not your Lord?" and they reply, "Yes, we witness it."

projection - the psychological process where one sees an inner quality of one's own as if it belonged to another person or thing

prana - the energy of life which connects the two worlds of inner and outer

remembrance - the Sufi practice of recollecting God in every breath and moment

safâ - purity of the heart

samâ' - sacred music or dance

samadhî - a spiritual state of awakened consciousness

service - the Sufi is a servant, is in service to the Beloved in this world, here for His sake

shadow - the darkness within, that of which one is unconscious in oneself, according to Carl Jung

shahâda - the central phrase of Islam and Sufism: *Lâ ilâha illâ Allâh*, there is no god but God. When used as a *dhikr*, this is often pronounced *Lâ ilâha illâ 'llâh*

sheikh - Sufi teacher

suhbat - spiritual relationship between master and disciple

sûf - wool

Sûra - verse, Qur'anic verse

tarîqa - one of the various Sufi orders or spiritual systems

tauba - the turning of the heart toward God

Throne - Sufi term referring to the Divine, as experienced by the human being

transformation - the alchemical process by which the lead of one's nature becomes the true gold

Upanishads - esoteric appendices to the various Vedas, Hindu scriptures

veils - the coverings of the heart which separate us from its consciousness, which is also His consciousness

via negativa - the path of unknowing, the mystical path to God and in God

walî - saint

wine - the intoxication of sweetness that the lover of God experiences in the love affair with the Beloved

INDEX

ACKNOWLEDGMENTS

For permission to use copyrighted material, the author gratefully wishes to acknowledge: Omega Publications, for permission to quote from a poem by Abû Saîd ibn Abî'l-Khayr printed in *The Drunken Universe: An Anthology of Persian Sufi Poetry*, translation and commentary ©1987 by Peter Lamborn Wilson and Nasrollah Pourjavady, and for permission to quote from *Rumi: Fragments, Ecstasies*, ©1981 by Daniel Liebert, Omega Publications Edition; HarperCollins Publishers, Inc., for permission to quote fourteen lines from *Tao Te Ching by Lao Tzu: A New English Version,* with foreword and notes by Stephen Mitchell, translation ©1988 by Stephen Mitchell; The Theosophical Publishing House, for permission to quote from *Perfume of the Desert: Inspirations from Sufi Wisdom,* compiled by Andrew Harvey and Eryk Hanut; Liveright Publishing Corporation, for permission to quote the lines from "silently if,out of not knowable" Copyright © 1963, 1991 by the Trustees for the E. E. Cummings Trust, and the lines from "stand with your lover on the ending earth—" Copyright 1949, © 1977, 1991 by the Trustees for the E. E. Cummings Trust, from *Complete Poems: 1904–1962* by E. E. Cummings, edited by George J. Firmage; Paulist Press, Inc., for permission to quote from *Fakhruddîn 'Irâqî: Divine Flashes*, translation and introduction by William C. Chittick and Peter Lamborn, ©1982 by Paulist Press, Inc.; Jane Hirshfield, for permission to quote from "Let the ascetics sing of the garden

LLEWELLYN VAUGHAN-LEE, Ph.D., is a Sufi teacher in the Naqshbandiyya-Mujaddidiyya Sufi Order. Born in London in 1953, he has followed the Naqshbandi Sufi path since he was nineteen. In 1991 he moved to Northern California and founded The Golden Sufi Center (www.goldensufi.org). He has authored a series of books that give a detailed exploration of the stages of spiritual and psychological transformation experienced on the Sufi path, with a particular focus on the use of dreamwork as inner guidance on the journey. Since 2000 the focus of his writing and teaching has been on spiritual responsibility in our present time of transition, the awakening global consciousness of oneness, and spiritual ecology (www.workingwithoneness.org). He has also been featured in the TV series Global Spirit and was interviewed by Oprah Winfrey as a part of her Super Soul Sunday series.

THE GOLDEN SUFI CENTER publishes books, video, and audio on Sufism and mysticism. A California 501(c)(3) religious nonprofit corporation, it is dedicated to making the teachings of the Naqshbandi Sufi path available to all seekers. For further information about the activities and publications, please contact:

THE GOLDEN SUFI CENTER
P.O. Box 456
Point Reyes Station, CA 94956-0456
tel: 415-663-0100 · fax: 415-663-0103
www.goldensufi.org